CONCEPTS FROM

PHYSICAL

AND

INORGANIC CHEMISTRY

(FOR UNDERGRADUATE STUDENTS)

Author

Kanchan R. Damade

(CSIR-NET-JRF, SET), Assistant Professor, Department of Chemistry Arts, Commerce and Science College, Bodwad Dist- Jalgaon, Maharashtra, India

Affiliated to Kaviyatri Bahinabai Chaudhari North Maharashtra University, Jalgaon, Maharashtra, India

AkiNik Publications
New Delhi

Published By: *AkiNik Publications*

AkiNik Publications
169, C-11, Sector - 3,
Rohini, Delhi-110085, India
Toll Free (India) – 18001234070
(National Level Publisher)

Author: *Kanchan R. Damade*

1st Edition: *2018*

Pages: *101*

ISBN: *978-93-5335-070-3*

Price: *₹425/-*

Preface

This book has developed as a notes for the Undergraduate students of chemistry framed by **Kaviyatri Bahinabai Chaudhary North Maharashtra University Jalgaon.** This study material serves a number of goals. The first goal is to form solid foundation of students of basic chemistry for further study in chemical sciences. However, knowledge of chemical sciences is becoming increasingly important in a much wider range of pharmaceuticals, research and engineering disciplines. Therefore, a second goal is to provide basic knowledge of chemistry to those students who belong to rural areas who do not get required guidance, will take a benefit from studying this book in chemistry through the conceptual tools that are used in designing this notes. Finally, a more pervasive goal is to expose all students not only to learn concepts but also to make intellectually rich foundations of the chemical sciences essential in qualifying various competitive examinations like CSIR-NET/SET and GATE.

This would be the first version of these study material and I will be in continuous practice for making updates in concepts included in this book. The main features of the present book are:

1. The seven chapters from physical and inorganic chemistry are included to meet demands of thousands of students of chemistry from all over India. Each chapter in these notes is made more elaborate by induction of colourful images made in M.S. Paint and some are downloaded from the various websites.
2. The book also explains to how to solve numerical problems from physical chemistry part.
3. The Multiple choice question are given to check there knowledge gain.
4. The text in the book presented in multicolour is to highlights the key points as well as to increase clarity, understand ability and legibility especially to those complex topics which cannot to assume by the inexperienced minds of competing students.

I express my gratitude to my family, friends and students who gave useful suggestions in preparing this book. The biggest thank is due to my Parents Shri Ramsingh K. Damade and Sau. Kusum Damade for keeping blessings always with me. I thank my brothers and sisters Arpana and

Khushabu who are real potential of mine. I pay my sincere thanks to Our Principal Hon. Professor Arvind Chaudhari who has noticed my efforts and encouraged me to publish this notes in book form. I express my sincere thanks to my college Management Body "**The Bodwad Sar. Co-Op. Education Society Ltd. Bodwad**" for providing me the platform to present this book for the students of chemistry in our country. Last but not least my sincere thanks to publishing team from Akinik publication, New Delhi who has taken their keen interest in printing and marketing of this book.

Kanchan R. Damade

The Bodwad Sarv.Co-op.Education Society Ltd.Bodwad
Arts,Commerce and Science College,Bodwad Dist - Jalgaon
NAAC Reaccredited 'B' Grade ISO - 9001:2008 (QMS)
Principal - Professor Arvind Chaudhari M.Com.M.Phil.Ph.D.
Tal - Bodwad, Dist - Jalgaon, Pin - 425 310, (M.S) India Office - 02582-276331 Fax - 02582-275268
www.acsbodwadcollege.org Email - bsces_accb@rediffmail.com

Outward No.: ACSCB/ / Date : 03/11/2018

Massage by Principal

I, am extremely happy for giving massage to the book published by my faculty member Smt.Kanchan Damade, Department of Chemistry. She has published the reference book titled **Concepts from Physical and Inorganic Chemistry** for the Under Graduate students. I hope the students refer said book and upgrade themselves in the particulare subject.

She add very useful subjective information for students, she has used simple language which students can understand easily.

I congratulate Smt.Kanchan Damade for her first publication.

Bodwad Dist.Jalgaon • Arts,Com.and Sci.College •

Professor Arvind Chaudhari
Principal

This Study Material is

dedicated to

My Mother..........

Contents

(Syllabus Framed by)

Kaviyatri Bahinabai Chaudhari North Maharashtra University, Jalgaon

Part - I Physical Chemistry

1. **Colligative Properties**

- Introduction,
- Lowering of vapor pressure of solvent,
- Calculation of molecular weight of solute from Lowering of vapor pressure of solvent.
- Boiling point elevation of solution,
- Calculation of molecular weight of solute from boiling point elevation of solution,
- Freezing point depression of solution,
- Calculation of molecular weight of solute from depression in Freezing point,
- Osmosis and osmotic pressure,
- Relation of osmotic pressure to vapour pressure,
- Van't –Hoff equation for osmotic pressure,
- Landberger's method for the determination of elevation of boiling point,
- Beckman's method for determination of depression in freezing point,
- Berkley and Hearty's method,
- Solution of electrolyte,
- Colligative properties of electrolyte (Qualitative concept only),
- Related numerical.

2. **Electrochemistry**

- Introduction,
- Electromotive force and its measurements,
- Standard cell,
- Cell reaction and EMF,
- convention regarding sign of EMF,
- Single electrode potential,
- Standard hydrogen and calomel reference electrodes,
- Calculation of single electrode potential,
- Calculation of cell EMF from single electrode potential,
- Thermodynamics and EMF, ΔG, ΔH, ΔS from EMF data,
- Thermodynamics of electrode potential (Nernst equation),
- Standard potential and equilibrium constant,
- Classification of electrodes,
- Related numericals.

Part-II Inorganic Chemistry

3. **Chemistry of Lanthanides Elements**

- Electronic Structure.
- Oxidation States.
- Extraction from monazite sand with flow sheet and Uses.
- Lanthanoid contraction – Definition, Causes, effects of lanthanoid contraction on chemistry of.
- Lanthanides & post lanthanoid elements.
- Separation of Lanthanides from one another by solvent extraction & ion exchange.
- Chromatography.

4. **Chemistry of Actinoids Elements**

- Electronic structure b. Position in periodic table.
- Oxidation states d. Occurrence of actinoids.
- Preparation of actinoids using.

a. Neutron bombardment.

b. Accelerated projectile bombardment.

c. Heavy ion bombardment.

5. Molecular Orbital Theory (MOT)

- Molecular orbital method.
- LCAO method.
- S-s, s-p, p-p, p-d & d-d combination of orbitals.
- Non Bonding combination of orbitals.
- Rules for linear combination of orbitals.
- Molecular orbital treatment for Homo nuclear Diatomic species- H_2, He_2, He_2^+, Li_2, Be_2, B_2, N_2 & F_2
- Molecular orbital treatment for Hetero nuclear diatomic molecules CO, NO, & HCl.

6. Chemistry of Transition Elements

- Elements of first, second & third transition series.
- General characteristics of d-block elements.

  a. Metallic character.

  b. Molar volume & densities.

  c. Atomic radii

  d. Ionic Radii

  e. Melting & boiling points

  f. Ionization Energies

  g. Reactivity

  h. Oxidation states

  i. Standard electrode potential

  j. Reducing properties

  k. Color

  l. Magnetic properties

  m. Catalytic Properties

  n. Tendency to form complexes.

7. The Metallic Bond

a. General Properties of Metals.

b. Conducivity, Luster, Malleability & cohesive force.

c. Conductors, Insulators & Semiconductors, Intrinsic & Exitrinsic semiconductors.

Chapter - 1

Colligative Properties

Introduction

Solute and solvent homogenous mixture is called as solution.

That is, Solute + solvent = solution

The colligative properties are concerned with the electrolytes as well as non-electrolytes solutions. The properties which depends on the concentrations of the solutions are included in colligative properties like boiling points, freezing points, vapour pressure and osmotic pressure.

To understand the various colligative properties we should consider the example of solution which contains nonvolatile solute particles.

E.g. consider a solution prepared by dissolving 5.00 g of NaCl in 100 g of pure water at 25°C and 1 atm pressure. The following table summarizes some of the differences in the properties of pure water and the NaCl solution.

A Comparison of Some of the Properties of Pure Water and an Aqueous NaCl Solution

Property	Pure Water	NaCl Solution
vapor pressure	23.8 torr	23.1 torr
boiling point	100.0°C	100.8°C
freezing point	0.0°C	-3.0°C
osmotic pressure	0.0 atm	33 atm

Source: http://www.chemelting pointurdue.edu

Colligative Properties

Definition-

The properties of a solution mainly depends on the number of particles of solute and not on the nature of solute are called colligative properties.

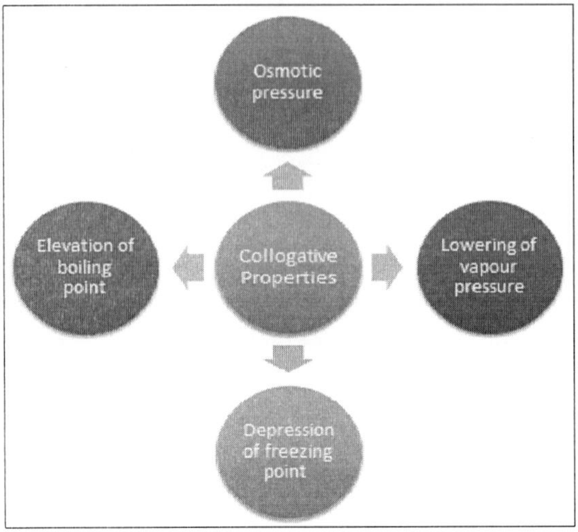

There are four colligative properties–

1. Lowering of vapour pressure of solvent
2. Elevation in boiling point of solution
3. Depression in freezing point of solution
4. Osmotic pressure.

Lowering of Vapour Pressure

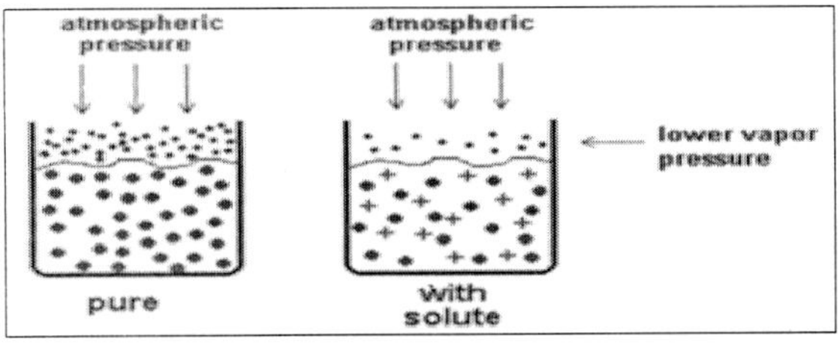

Source: https://www.youtube.com

If nonvolatile solute dissolve in a solvent, then vapour pressure of solution get lowers.

This lowering of vapour pressure is explained by Raoult's law-

Raoult's law-

''Partial vapour pressure of Any Volatile Component of a Solution is Equal to the Product of vapour pressure of Pure Component and Mole Fraction of That Component IN the Solution.''

Let, solvent-1 and solute-2 are the component of the solution.

So, N_1 - mole fraction of the solvent.

N_2 - mole fraction of the solute

P0 - pure solvent vapour pressure

P- Partial vapour pressure of solution

By Raoult's law-

$P= P^0 N_1$

N_1 is less than one, therefore $P < P^0$

Lowering of Vapour Pressure (ΔP)-

When nonvolatile solvent is added into solvent, the VAPOUR PRESSURE of solvent decreases.

"The difference between in vapour pressure of pure solvent and solution is known as lowering in Vapour Pressure of solution."

$\Delta P = P^0 - P$ ...1

Where, P^0 – pure solvent vapour pressure

P- vapour pressure of solution

From Raoult's law,

$P= P^0 N_1$ ...2

Putting 2 in 1

$\Delta P = P^0 - P^0 N_1$

$\Delta P = P^0 (1 - N_1)$ ...3

$N_1 + N_2 = 1$

Therefore, $1 - N_1 = N_2$ ...4

Putting 4 in 3

$\Delta P = P^0 N_2$

Relative Lowering in vapour pressure ($\Delta p/p^0$)

This lowering in V.P depends on vapour pressure of pure solvent and mole fraction of solute (N2), i.e number of solute particles.

Therefore lowering in V.P is a colligative property.

Definition

"The ratio of lowering in **vapour pressure** ΔP to the **vapour pressure** of pure solvent (P^0) is called as relative lowering in **vapour pressure** "Ionisation energy.

Relative lowering in V.P= $\Delta p/p^0$

But, $\Delta P = P^0 - P$

Hence, $\Delta P/P = P^0 - P/ P^0 = N_2$

Thus relative lowering in **vapour pressure** is depends on mole fraction of solute ionisation energy. Number of solute particles. Therefore it is colligative properties.

Calculation of Molecular Weight of Solute by Lowering in vapour pressure of Solvent

The Relative lowering in **vapour pressure** = $\Delta P/P^0$

$$\Delta P/ P^0 = P^0 - P/P = N$$

If n_1 and n_2 are number of moles of solvent and solute respectively.

Therefore,

$$N_2 = n_2 / n_1 + n_2$$

$$\Delta P/P^0 = (P^0 - P)/ P = n2 / n1 + n2$$

But solution is very dilute therefore, $n2 <<< n1$

$$n1 + n2 \equiv n1$$

Therefore,

$$\Delta P/P^0 = n2 /n1$$

W1 and W2 are the weight of solvent and solute,

M1 and M2 are the molecular weight of solvent and solute respectively.

$$\frac{\Delta P}{P^0} = \frac{W2/ M2}{W1/M1}$$

$$\frac{\Delta P}{P^0} = \frac{W2 \times M1}{M2 \times W1}$$

$$\Delta P = \frac{W2 \times M1 \times P^0}{M2 \times W1}$$

If W1, W2, M1 is known to us, than we can calculate (M2) molecular weight of solute.

Boiling Point Elevation of Solution

The difference in boiling point of solvent (To) and that of the solution (T) is called elevation in boiling point of solution

When non-volatile solute is dissolved in volatile solvent, then the BOILING POINT increases. This elevation in boiling point, depends on number of solute particles.

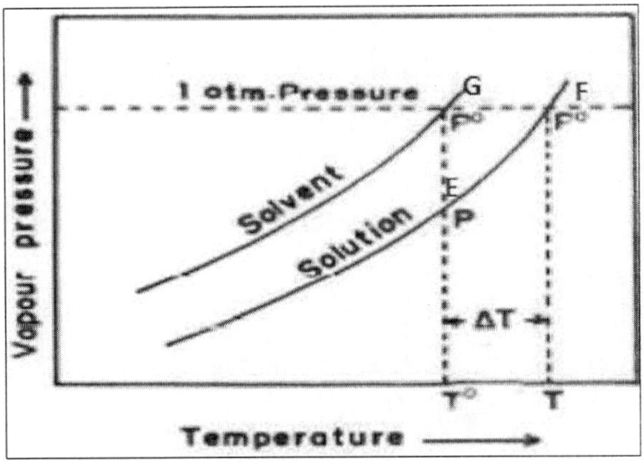

Source: https://onlinechemistryhelp.wordpress.com

P^0 = **vapour pressure** of pure solvent

P= **vapour pressure** of solution

To= boiling point of solvent

T = boiling point of solution

ΔTb= T- To

ΔTb = elevation in Boiling point

By applying Clausius Clapeyorn equation to curve EF

$\ln P^0/P = \Delta Hv / R\,[(T - To)/TTo]$

Where,

R = molar gas constant

ΔHv = heat of vapourisation

As solution is very dilute there is small difference in T and to

Therefore,

$$T\text{-}To \equiv to \;\&$$

$$T\text{-}To \equiv To^2$$

Then,

$$\ln P^0/P = \Delta Hv\ \underline{\Delta Tb}/RTo^2$$

Rearranging above equation,

$\ln P/P^0 = RTo^2/\Delta Hv\ (\Delta Tb)$ ...1

From Raoults law,

$P= P^0 N_1$

$P/P_0 = N_1$

But $N_1 = 1\text{-}N_2$

Therefore, $P/P_0 = 1\text{-}N_2$

Taking log on both side,

$\ln P/P_0 = \ln 1\text{-}N_2$ ...2

According to Maclaurins theorem,

$$\ln (1\text{-}N_2) = \underline{-N_2 - N_2^2 - N_2^3 - N_2^4} \ldots\ldots\ldots\ldots$$

$$2! \quad 3! \quad 4!$$

Since, N2 I very small, all the terms are neglected except –N2

$\ln 1\text{-}N_2 = -N_2$ ...3

Comparing 2 and 3

$\ln P/P^0 = -N2$ ...4

Rearranging equation 4

$\ln P^0 /P = N_2$ ...5

Comparing equation 1 and 5

$N_2 = R\ To^2/\Delta Hv\ (\Delta Tb)$

$$\mathbf{\Delta Tb = (R \times T^2_0/\Delta Hv)\ N2}$$

All Terms in Bracket are Constant. Hence it is Proved That Elevation in Boiling Point are Colligative Property That it depends on Number of Solute Particles.

In the study of colligative property, concentration is not expressed in mole fraction but in terms of molality (m).

Let, m be the number of moles of solute in 1000g of solvent.

$N_2 = \underline{m/}\ m+n_1$

But solution is dilute m<<< n1 therefore m+n1≡ n1

$N_2 = m/n1$

Substitute above equation in 6

$\Delta Tb = (R\ To^2/\Delta Hv)\ \underline{m/}\ n_1$

$\Delta Tb = (R\ To^2/\Delta Hv.\ n_1)\ \underline{m}$

Where, $(R\ To^2/\Delta Hv.\ n_1) = Kb$

Therefore equation 7 becomes-

$\Delta Tb = Kb \times m$

When m=1, then $\Delta Tb = Kb$

Definition –

" **The elevation in boiling point, when one mole of solute is dissolved in 1000g of solvent, is called as Ebullioscopic constant.**

Latent heat of vapourisation and ebullioscopic constant Kb-We know,

$n1 = W1/M1$

Here weight of solvent is 1000 gm

$n1 = 1000/M1$

Since,

$\Delta Hv/M1$ = latent heat of vaporization Lv

$(R\ To^2/\Delta Hv.\ n_1) = Kb$

$[R\ To^2/\Delta Hv.\ (1000/M1)] = Kb$

$(R\ To^2/\ (\Delta Hv/M1).\ 1000) = Kb$

But, $\Delta Hv/M1$ = [Lv Latent heat of vapourisation]

$$\mathbf{Kb = R \times To^2/Lv.\ 1000}$$

Calculation of Molecular Weight from Elevation of Boiling Point-

The elevation in boiling point of solution is given by-

$\Delta Tb = Kb \times m$ ...1

We have,

m = weight of solute/molecular weight of solute

But weight of solute in 1000gm of solvent is given by,

$= W_2 \times 1000/W_1$

W_1 = weight of solvent

W_2 = weight of solute

Therefore,

m = weight of solute per 1000 gm/molecular weight of solute

$m = [W_2 \times 1000/W_1]/M_2$ ...2

Substituting 2 in 1

$\Delta Tb = Kb \times W_2 \times 1000/W_1 \times M_2$

Rearranging above equation,

$$M_2 = Kb \times W_2 \times 1000/\Delta Tb \times W_1$$

Using above formula we can calculate the molecular weight of solute.

Landsberger's Method for Determination of Elevation of Boiling Point-

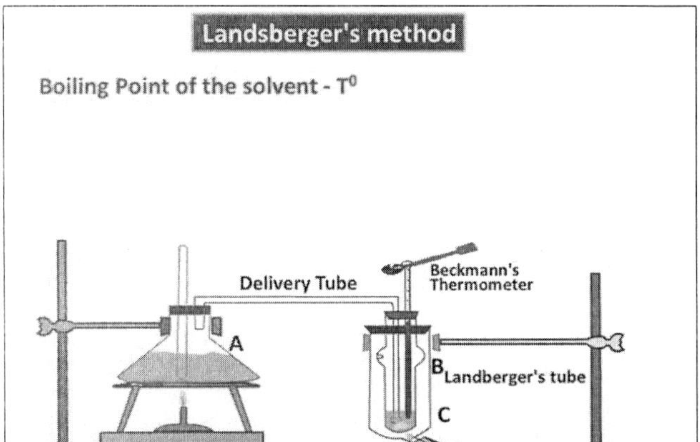

The landsberger's methods is useful for determination of elevation of boiling point which is useful to calculate the molecular weight of non-volatile solute.

The elevation of boiling point is obtained by measuring boiling point of Solvent (T) and boiling point of solution (T^0).

The apparatus is shown in fig.

Construction

This apparatus consist a conical flask A which is filled by solvent. This flask is then connected with delivery tube and safety tube. The Landsberger's tube B is calliberated from the bottom to measure volume in ml. This tube has a bulb at the middle and with one hole to escape the excess vapours. This tube is fitted with double hole cork, from one of the hole it is connected with delivery tube and from the another hole Beckmenns thermometer is inserted. The whole tube is covered with outer jacket which is connected with condenser C to condense the excess vapours.

Working

The conical flask which is filled with solvent (water) is heated through the burner which forms hot vapour. The known amount of volume of solvent is filled in tube-B. The hot vapours then passes through the delivery tube and enter into the tube –B. these hot vapour now heat the solvent of tube-B and at particular temperature it starts boiling. The temperature is accurately measured by Beckmenn's thermometer. This is the boiling point of pure solvent (T_0).

Similarly we can record the boiling point of solution (T) also by adding known amount of solute in tube-B.

By finding out difference between of boiling point of solution and pure solvent we can calculate the elevation in boiling point solution.

$$\Delta Tb = T - To$$

After calculating the elevation in boiling point we can calculate the molecular weight of solute by using formula-

$$M_2 = Kb \times W_2 \times 1000 / \Delta Tb \times W_1$$

W_1 = weight of solvent

W_2 = weight of solute

Kb= molal elevation constant.

M= molecular weight of solute

Depression in Freezing Point of Solution

Freezing point depression is a colligative property observed in solutions that results from the introduction of solute molecules to a solvent. The freezing points of solutions are all lower than that of the pure solvent.

$\Delta Tf = Tf\,(\text{solvent}) - Tf\,(\text{solution})$

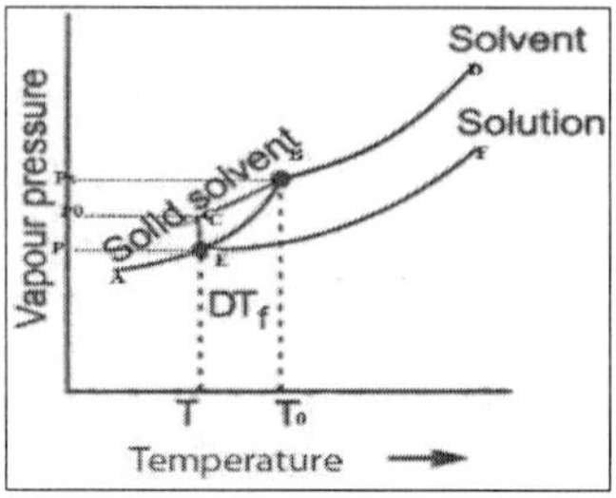

Source: http://www.sciencehq.com

The vapour pressure –temperature diagram for studying depression in freezing point of solution is shown in fig.

AB = sublimation curve of solid solvent

CD= Vapour pressure curve of pure solvent

At freezing point of pure solvent T_0, the solid and liquid phases have identical vapour pressure P_S.

P is the vapour pressure of solvent in solution at temperature T.

P^0 is the vapour pressure of super cooled liquid at temperature T.

Applying Clausius Clapeyorn equation to curve CB.

$\ln P_s/P^0 = \Delta Hv/R\ [(To- T)/TTo]$ ...1

Where,

R = molar gas constant

ΔHv = heat of vapourisation

Similarly, applying Clausius Clapeyorn equation to curve EB

$\ln P_s/P = \Delta Hs/R\ [(To- T)/TTo]$ ...2

ΔHs = heat of sublimation of solid solvent.

By substracting 2 from 1

$[\ln P_s/P^0 - \ln P_s/P] = [\Delta Hv/R - \Delta Hs/R]\ [(To-T)/TTo]$

$\ln P_s/P^0 \times P/P_s = [(\Delta Hv - \Delta Hs)/R]\ [(To-T)/TTo]$

By putting $(\Delta Hv - \Delta Hs) = -(\Delta Hs - \Delta Hv)$

Therefore,

$\ln P/P^0 = -[(To- T)/R\ TTo]\ (\Delta Hs - \Delta Hv)$ ...3

But,

a. $(\Delta Hs - \Delta Hv) = \Delta H_f$

b. $(To- T) = \Delta T_f$

c. $T\text{-}To = To^2$ (since, $T\text{-}To \equiv To$ & $TTo \equiv To^2$)

From a, b, c …Eq. 3 becomes,

$\ln P/P^0 = - \Delta T_f \Delta H_f//R\ To^2$ …4

From Raoults law,

$P= P^0 N_1$

$P/P_0 = N_1$

But $N_1 = 1\text{-}N_2$

Therefore, $P/P_0 = 1\text{-}N_2$

Taking log on both sides,

$\ln P/P_0 = \ln 1\text{-}N_2$ …5

According to Maclaurins theorem,

$\ln (1\text{-}N_2) = -N_2 - \frac{N_2^2}{2!} - \frac{N_2^3}{3!} - \frac{N_2^4}{4!}$ ……….

Since, N_2 is very small, all the terms are neglected except $-N_2$

$\ln 1\text{-}N_2 = -N_2$ …6

Comparing 5 and 6…

$\ln P/P^0 = -N_2$ …7

Comparison of Eq-4 and Eq-7 will give….

$-N_2 = - \Delta T_f \Delta H_f /R\ To^2$

$\Delta T_f = [RTo^2/\Delta H_f]\ N_2$ …8

All Terms in Bracket Are Constant, so Equation-8 Concludes That ''The Depression In Freezing Point of Solution is Depends on Mole Fraction of Solute That is Number of Solute Particles Hence it IS Colligative Properties.''

In the study of colligative property, concentration is not expressed in mole fraction but in terms of molality (m).

Let, m be the number of moles of solute in 1000g of solvent.

$N_2 = \underline{m}/m+n_1$

But solution is dilute m<<< n1 therefore m+n1≡ n1

$N_2 = m/n1$

Substitute above equation in 8

$\Delta T_f = (R\,To^2/\Delta H_f)\,\underline{m/n_1}$

$\Delta T_f = (R\,To^2/\Delta H_f/n_1)\,m$

Where, $(R\,To^2/\Delta H_f/n_1) = K_f$

K_f = cryoscopic constant or molal freezing point constant

Therefore equation 8 becomes-

$\Delta T_f = K_f \times m$

When m=1, then $\Delta T_f = K_f$

Definition –

" **The depression in freezing point, when one mole of solute is dissolved in 1000g of solvent, is called as cryoscopic constant or molal freezing point constant.**

Latent Heat of Fusion and Cryoscopic Constant (K_f) -

We know,

$n_1 = W_1/ M_1$

Here weight of solvent is 1000 gm

$n_1 = 1000/ M_1$

Since,

$\Delta Hf/ M_1$ = latent heat of fusion (Lf)

$K_f = (R\,To^2/\Delta H_f/n_1)$

$K_f = [R\,To^2/\Delta H_f.\,(1000/M_1)]$

$K_f = [R\,To^2/\,(\Delta H_f/M_1)\,1000]$

But, $\Delta H_f./M_1= L_f$ (Latent heat of fusion)

$K_f = [R\,To^2/L_f \times 1000]$

Calculation of Molecular Weight from Depression of Freezing Point-

The elevation in boiling point of solution is given by –

$\Delta T_f = K_f \times m$ ...1

We have,

m = weight of solute/molecular weight of solute

But weight of solute in 1000gm of solvent is given by,

$= W_2 \times 1000/W_1$

W_1 = weight of solvent

W_2 = weight of solute

Therefore,

m = weight of solute per 1000 gms / molecular weight of solute

$m = [W_2 \times 1000/W_1]/M_2$ ...2

Substituting 2 in 1

$\Delta T_f = K_f \times W_2 \times 1000/W_1 \times M_2$

Rearranging above equation,

$$\mathbf{M_2 = K_f \times W_2 \times 1000/\Delta T_f \times W_1}$$

Using above formula we can calculate the molecular weight of solute.

Numericals

Example-1

1.60 g of naphthalene ($C_{10}H_8$) is dissolved in 20.0 g of benzene. The freezing point of pure benzene is 5.5 °C, and the freezing point of the mixture is 2.8 °C. What is the molal freezing point depression constant, K_f of benzene?

Solution-

We have,

Solute- naphthalene

Solvent = benzene

Step 1: Calculate the freezing point depression of benzene.

$\Delta Tf = Tf\,(solvent) - Tf\,(solution)$

$2.7°C = (5.5°C) - (2.8°C)$

Step 2: Calculate the molal concentration of the solution.

Molality = moles of solute/kg of solvent

Moles of naphthalene = Weight of naphthalene/ molecular weight

= (1.60g/128g)

= 0.0125 mol naphthalene

Molality of solution = (0.0125 mol) / (0.0200 kg)

= 0.625 m

Step 3: Calculation K_f of the solution.

$\Delta T_f = K_f \times m$

$2.7°C = K_f \times 0.625$ m

$K_f = 4.3°C/m$

Example - 2

Calculate the Mass of Ascorbic Acid (Vitamin C, $C_6H_8O_6$) to be dissolved in 75 g of Acetic Acid to lower its Melting Point by 1.5°C. K_b = 3.9 K kg mol^{-1}.

Solution-

Mass of acetic acid, w_1= 75g

Molar mass of ascorbic acid ($C_6H_8O_6$)

$M_2 = 6 \times 12 + 8 \times 1 + 6 \times 16 = 176$ g mol^{-1}

Lowering of melting point, $\Delta T_b = 1.5$ K

$$\Delta T_b = \frac{k_b \times 1000 \times w_2}{M_2 \times w_1}$$

$$w_2 = \frac{\Delta T_b \times M_2 \times w_1}{1000 \times k_b}$$

= (1.5 x 176 x 75)/(3.9 x 1000)

= 5.08 g (approx)

Hence, 5.08 g of ascorbic acid is needed to be dissolved.

Measurement of Freezing Point Depression by Beckmann Method

A simple Beckmann apparatus is shown in fig. It consists of a freezing tube with a side arm through which a known amount of a solute can be introduced. A stopper carrying a Beckmann thermometer and a stirrer is fitted in to the freezing tube. To prevent rapid cooling of the contents of the freezing tube and an outer tube (e) surrounds the tube so that there is an air jacket between tube and outer jacket. This assembly, as a whole, is placed in a wide vessel which contains a freezing mixture maintaining a low temperature around 5°C below the freezing point of the pure solvent.

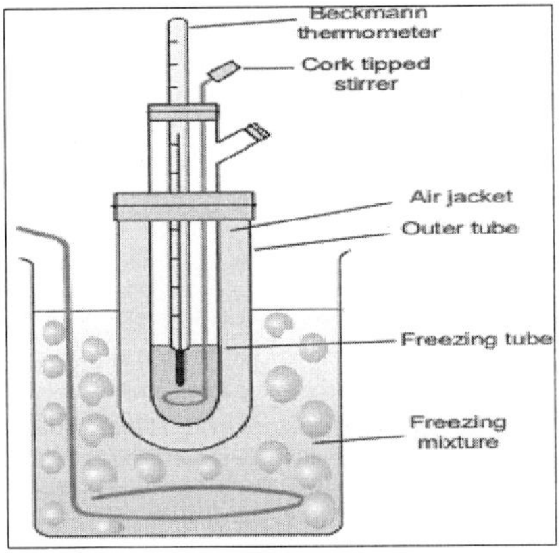

Fig: Beckmann's apparatus

A known weight of the pure solvent is placed in the freezing tube. It is cooled with gentle and continuous stirring. As a result of super cooling, the temperature of the solvent will fall by about 0.5 ^{0}C below its freezing point. Vigorous stirring is then set in when solid starts separating and the temperature rises to the exact freezing point. This temperature remains constant, for some time, until all the liquid solvent gets solidified and is noted as T°.

The freezing tube is taken out, warmed to melt the solid and a known weight of the solute is added through the side arm. When the solute is dissolved in to the solvent forming a solution, the tube is put back in to the original position and the freezing point of the solution (T) is re determined in the same manner as before. The difference between the two readings gives the freezing point depression (ΔTf).

Depression in freezing point ΔTf = T°-T.

From this value, the molecular mass of the non-volatile solute can be determined using the expression and known Kf value.

$$\mathbf{M_2 = K_f \times W_2 \times 1000/\Delta T_f \times W_1}$$

Osmosis and Osmotic Pressure

Osmosis

Definition

A process by which molecules of a solvent tend to pass through a semipermeable membrane from a less concentrated solution into a more concentrated one.

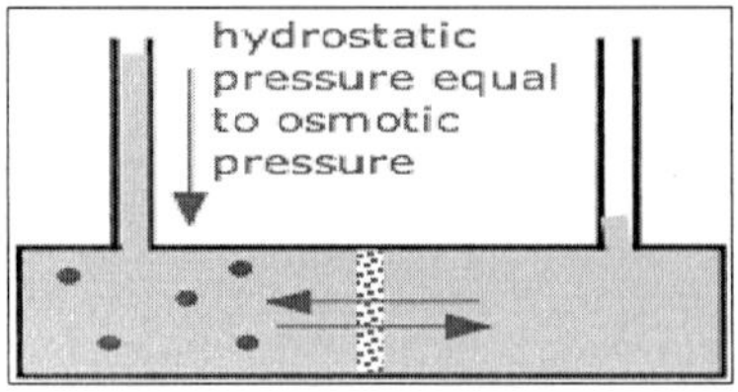

In these experiment there are two compartments contains water, but the left compartment contains a solute whose molecules (represented by blue circles) are too large to pass through the membrane. Many artificial and natural substances are capable of acting as semi-permeable membranes. The walls of most plant and animal cells fall into this category.

In the setup, the liquid level is initially the same in both compartments, soon the liquid rises in the left compartment and falls in the right side, indicating that water molecules from the right compartment are migrating through the semipermeable membrane into left compartment. This migration of the solvent is known as osmotic flow, or simply osmosis.

Osmotic Pressure

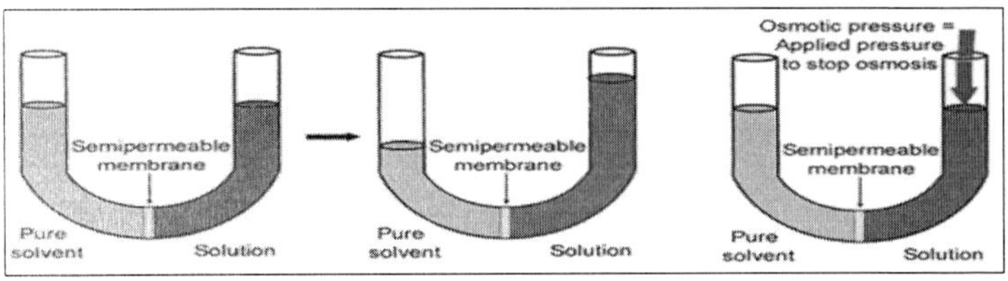

Definition

Osmotic pressure is the pressure required to stop osmosis.

U-Tube Showing Osmotic Pressure

On the left side of the U-tube is pure solvent, and on the right side is aqueous solution. The pure water is trying to dilute the solution by travelling through the semipermeable membrane. Eventually the addition of extra molecules of solvent on the right causes increase in the level of liquid at solution side. By applying the external pressure on solution side through piston the original level of solution is attained. This external pressure applied to stop the osmosis is called osmotic pressure.

Osmotic pressure is the pressure that needs to be applied to a solution to prevent the flow of solvent molecules through a semipermeable membrane. Osmotic pressure can also be explained as the pressure is essential to stop osmosis. The osmotic pressure is the pressure required to achieve osmotic equilibrium.

Berkeley-Hartley Method to Determine Osmotic Pressure

The apparatus used is shown in Fig.

A porcelain tube having copper ferrocyanide as a semipermeable membrane in its walls is enclosed in a metallic jacket. The porcelain tube is fitted with a reservoir of pure solvent at one end and a capillary tube at the other end. In a metallic jacket there is an arrangement for applying external pressure which is measured with the help of pressure gauge.

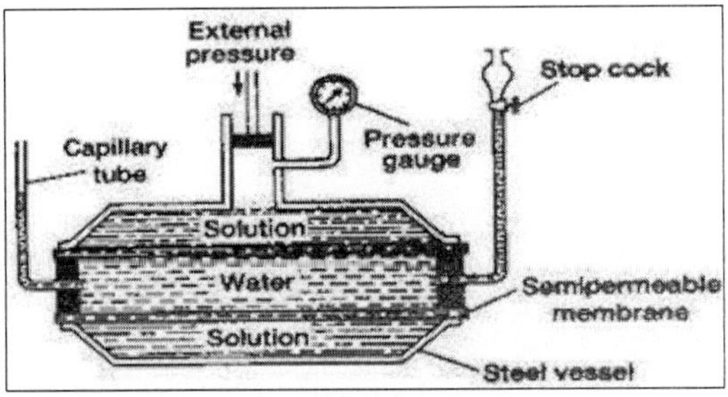

Procedure: The porcelain tube is filled with pure solvent (water) and the metallic jacket with solution. The level in the capillary tube will tend to move down as the solvent flows towards solution due to osmosis. External pressure is now applied on the solution by the piston so that level in capillary remains stationary. The reading of pressure gauge is recorded. This is the osmotic pressure of the solution.

Relation of Osmotic Pressure to Vapour Pressure

This relationship of Osmotic pressure with vapour pressure is obtained by using thermodynamics parameters.

Let G^0_1 is the molal free energy of pure solvent.

G_1 is the molal free energy of solvent in solution

So, the difference in G^0_1 and G_1 is given as,

We know,

$G^0_1 > G_1$

Where the osmosis is spontaneous process therefore the free energy change is accompanied by decrease in free energy.

$G_1 - G^0_1 = -\Delta G$ ...1

The partial molal free energy of any component in solution is given by,

$G_1 = G^0_1 + RT\ln a_1$

Where,

R= molar gas constant

T = Temperature in absolute.

a_1 = activity of the component of solution.

$G_1 - G^0_1 = RT\ln a_1$

But,

$a_1 = P_1/P_1^0$

Therefore,

$G_1 - G^0_1 = RT\ln P_1/P_1^0$

From Eq-1

$-\Delta G = RT\ln P_1/P_1^0$

Therefore,

$\Delta G = RT\ln P_1^0/P_1$ ...2

But the partial molal free energy changes in terms of partial molal volume, which is given as

$dG_1 = V'_1\, dp$

V'_1 = Partial molal volume of solvent in solution

Integrating above equation with in a limit of partial molal free energy from G_1 to G_1^1 and pressure in between 1 to P

$\int_{G1}^{G'1} dG1 = \int_1^P V1\, dp$

$[G_1]^{G'1}_{G1} = V1[P - 1]$ ...3

Where P-1 = pressure applied to stop osmosis.

Therefore P-1 = π = Osmotic pressure

And $G^1{}_1 - G_1 = \Delta G$

Therefore eq-3 becomes

$\Delta G = V1.\pi$ ...4

Comparing equation 4 and 2

$RT\ln P_1^0/P_1 = V1.\pi$

$\pi = (RT/V1)\ln P_1^0/P_1$ ...5

Eq-5 is the relation between osmotic pressure and vapour pressure.

$$\pi = (2.303RT/V1) \log_{10} P_1^0/P_1$$

When the solution is very dilute

$$V1 = V_1^0$$

V_1^0 = molar volume of pure solvent

$$\pi = (2.303\ RT/\ V_1^0) \log_{10} P_1^0/P_1 \qquad ...6$$

Eq-6 is used to calculate the osmotic pressure of solution if vapour pressure of solution and vapour pressure of pure solvent at temperature T is known.

Van't Hoff Equation for Osmotic Pressure

The osmotic pressure is related to vapour pressure by equation....

$$\pi = (2.303\ RT/\ V_1^0) \log_{10} P_1^0/P_1$$

V_1^0 = molar volume of pure solvent

By Raoult law,

$$P= P^0 N_1$$

$$P/P_0 = N_1$$

But $N_1 = 1\text{-}N_2$

Therefore, $P/P_0 = 1\text{-}N_2$ ...5

Where N_2 = is the mole fraction of solute.

We already know,

$$\pi = (RT/V_1^0) \ln P_1^0/P_1$$

$$\pi = -\ (RT/V_1^0) \ln P_1/P_1^0$$

By substituting value of $P_1/P_1{}^0$ from equation -5

$$\pi = -\ (RT/V_1^0) \ln 1\text{-}N_2 \qquad ...6$$

According to Maclaurins theorem,

$$\text{Ln}\ (1\text{-}N_2) = -N_2 - \frac{N_2^2}{2!} - \frac{N_2^3}{3!} - \frac{N_2^4}{4!} \ldots\ldots\ldots\ldots$$

Since, N_2 is very small; all the terms are neglected except $-N_2$

$$\text{Ln}\ 1\text{-}N_2 = -N_2$$

Now eq-6 becomes...

$\pi = - (RT/V_1^0) (-N_2)$

$\pi = (RT/V_1^0) N_2$

Then,

Let, n_1 be the number of moles of solute and n_2 is of solvent.

$N_2 = n_2/ n_2+n_1$

But solution is dilute $n_2 <<< n_1$ therefore $n_2+n_1 = n_1$

$N_2 = n_2/n_1$

$\pi = (RT/V_1^0) n_2/n_1$

$\pi V_1^0 n_1 = RT \times n_2$

But $V_1^0 n_1 = V$ total volume of solvent containing solute of n_2 moles.

$\pi V = RT \times n_2$

$\pi = RT \times n_2/V$

Where,

$n_2/V = C$ (concentration of solution)

Therefore,

$$\pi = RT \times n_2/V = RTC$$

Or

$$\boxed{\pi = CRT}$$

This equation is called as Van't Hoff equation.

Determination of Molecular Weight of Solute by Osmotic Pressure.

By Vant'hoff equation,

$\pi V = RT \times n_2$

If W_2 = Weight of solute in gram

M_2 = Molecular Weight of solute.

Then,

$n_2 = W_2/M_2$

Therefore,

$\pi V = RT \times W_2/M_2$

$M_2 = RT W_2/\pi V$

Using above equation we can calculate the molecular weight of solute.

Solution of Electrolyte

An electrolyte solution is a solution that generally contains ions, atoms or molecules that have lost or gained electrons, and is electrically conductive.

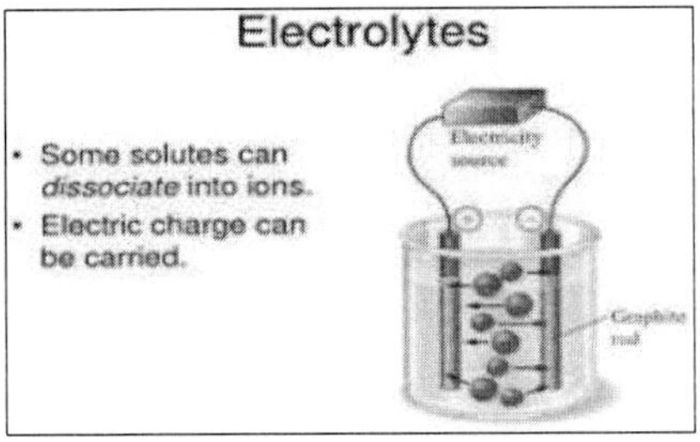

And the non-electrolyte are the solutions which cannot conduct the electricity as they have no free ions or hydrated ions, such as Ethyl alcohol and sugar solution.

The solution of non-electrolyte shows colligative properties. The molecular weight which has been calculated from colligative properties of non- electrolyte will be same as formula weight. This is because they have same number of solute particles after addition of solute in solvent.

But in some cases molecular weight obtained from colligative properties are different from that of formula weight, this is due to association or dissociation of solute particles.

Colligative Properties of Electrolytes

The colligative properties of solutions, viz. lowering of vapour pressure, osmotic pressure, elevation in boiling point and depression in freezing point, depend on the total number of solute particles present in solution. Since the electrolytes ionise and give more than one particle per formula unit in solution, the colligative effect of an electrolyte solution is always greater than that of a non-electrolyte of the same molar concentration. All colligative properties are used for calculating molecular masses of non-volatile solutes.

Colligative properties are depending on following factor-

In case of non-electrolytes

1) Colligative properties $\propto$ Number of particles (molecules)

In case of electrolytes

2) Colligative properties $\propto$ Number of ions

Van't Hoff Factor (*i*)

Since colligative properties depend upon the number of particles of the solute, in some cases where the solute associates or dissociates in solution, abnormal results for molecular masses are obtained.

Van't Hoff, in order to account for all abnormal cases introduced a factor **i** known as the *Van't Hoff factor*, such that

$$i = \frac{\text{Observed colligative property (actual)}}{\text{Theoretical colligative property (expected)}}$$

$$= \frac{\text{No. of molecules actually present}}{\text{No. of molecules expected to be present}}$$

Definition of Van't Hoff factor -

"The ratio of colligative effect produced by concentration m of electrolyte divided by the effect observed of non-electrolyte for the same concentration."

Applying this factor to various colligative properties-

$i = \Delta T_f/(\Delta T_f)o$

Where,

ΔT_f = depression in freezing point of electrolyte

$(\Delta T_f)o$ = depression in freezing point of non-electrolyte

Therefore,

$(\Delta T_f)o = K_f \times m$

Now,

$i = \Delta T_f/K_f \times m$

By knowing value of i, we can calculate the value of colligative properties for electrolytes.

Similarly we can write,

$i = \Delta T_f/(\Delta T_f)o = \Delta T_b/(\Delta T_b)o = \Delta P/(\Delta P)o = \pi/\pi_0$

1. **For Lowering in Vapour Pressure**

$i = \Delta P/(\Delta P)o$

Since,

$(\Delta P)o = P^0 N_2$

$\Delta P = i P^0 N_2$

2. **For Elevation in Boiling Point**

$i = \Delta T_b / (\Delta T_b)o$

Since,

$(\Delta T_b)o = K_b \times m$

Therefore,

$i = \Delta T_b / K_b \times m$

$\Delta T_b = i \times K_b \times m$

3. **Osmotic Pressure**

$i = \pi / \pi_0$

Therefore,

$\pi = i / \pi_0$

Since,

$(\pi)_0 = RT \times n_2/V$

$\pi = i \times RT \times n_2/V$

Abnormal Molecular Weight

Molecular masses of the solute can be easily determined with the help of colligative properties; relative lowering in vapour pressure, boiling point elevation, freezing point depression, and osmotic pressure easily. When molecules associate or dissociates the values of molecular weight are either too large or small.

This apparent molecular mass different from actual molecular mass are called as abnormal molecular weight or mass.

This is due to association or dissociation of particles -

Association

There are many organic solutes which in non-aqueous solutions undergo association, that is, two or more molecules of the solute associate to form a bigger molecule. Thus, the number of effective molecules decreases and, consequently the osmotic pressure, the elevation of boiling point or depression of freezing point, is less than that calculated on the basis of a single molecule.

Two examples are: acetic acid in benzene and chloroacetic acid in naphthalene.

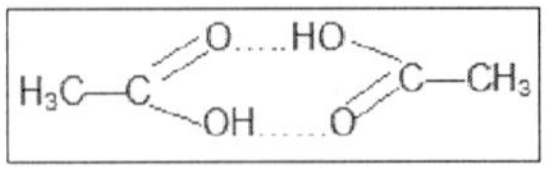

Association of Acetic acid in benzene through hydrogen bonding

Dissociation

Inorganic acids, bases and salts in aqueous solutions undergo dissociation, that is, the molecules break down into positively and negatively charged ions. In such cases, the number of *effective* particles increases and, therefore, osmotic pressure, elevation of boiling point and depression of freezing point are much higher than those calculated on the basis of an undissociated single molecule.

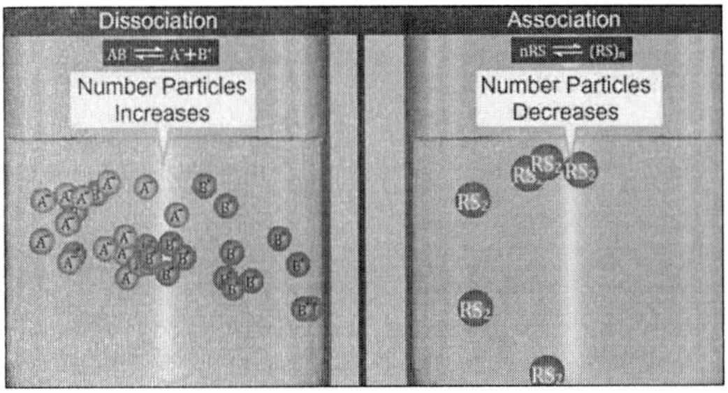

Numericals

Example-1

36 Grams of Glucose ($C_6H_{12}O_6$) is Dissolved in 1 kg of Water. At What Temperature Will the Water Boil at 1.013 bar? Kb for Water is 0.52 K kg Mol^{-1}.

Ans: (given weight of glucose) W_2 = 36 grams

(Given weight of water) W_1 = 1 kg= 1000 grams

(Molecular weight of glucose) M_2 = 180

K_b= 0.52

$\Delta T_b = (K_b \text{x} W_2 \text{x} 1000)/ (M_2 \text{x} W_1)$

$= (0.52 \text{x} 36 \text{x} 1000)/ (180 \text{x} 1000)$

= 0.104K

T_b°= 373.15 K at 1.013 bar

Water which contains 36 grams of glucose will boil at 373.15 K temperature.

$T_b = \Delta T_b + T_b°$

$= 373.15 + 0.104$

$Tb = 373.254K$

Example-2

When 92.0 g of a Molecular Compound was dissolved in 1000.G of Water, the Freezing Point of the Solution was lowered to -3.72 °c. What is the Molecular Weight of the Compound?

Solution:

$\Delta T = i\ K_f\ m$

$3.72\ °C = (1)\ (1.86\ °C\ kg\ mol^{-1})\ (x / 1.000\ kg)$

$3.72\ °C = (1.86\ °C\ mol^{-1})\ (x)$

$x = 2.00\ mol$

$92.0g / 2.00\ mol =$

$= 46.0\ g/mol$

Example-3

A Solution of 2.5 g of a Non-Volatile Solid in 100 g Benzene Boiled at 0.42°C Higher than the Boiling Point of Pure Benzene. Calculate the Molecular Mass of the Substance. Molal Elevation Constant of Benzene is 2.67 K kg mol^{-1}.

Solution

$m = 1000K_b \times W_2/W_1 \times \Delta T_b$

Given, $K_b = 2.67$,

$W_2 = 2.5$ g,

$W_1 = 100$ g,

$\Delta T_b = 0.42$

$m = 1000 \times 2.67 \times 2.5/100 \times 0.42 = 158.9$

The molecular mass of substance is 158.9.

Example - 4

By Dissolving 13.6 g of a Substance in 20 g of Water, the Freezing Point Decreased by 3.7°C. Calculate the Molecular Mass of the Substance. [Molal Depression Constant for Water = 1.863 K kg mol^{-1}]

Solution

$m = 1000K_b \times W_2/W_1 \times \Delta T_f$

Given, $K_f = 1.863$ K kg mol^{-1}.

$W_2 = 13.6$ g,

$W_1 = 20$ g,

$\Delta T_f = 3.7°C$

$M_2 = 1000 \times 1.863 \times 13.6/20 \times 3.7 = 243.39$

MCQ Practice

1. **Colligative properties depend only on**
   a. volume
   b. pressure
   c. temperature
   d. **number of particles**

2. **Which of the Following Alternatives Does not represent a Colligative Property?**
   a. Lowering of vapour pressure
   b. **Osmosis**
   c. Elevation of boiling point
   d. Depression of freezing point

3. **The Driving Force of Osmosis is**
   a. Osmotic pressure
   b. Vapour pressure
   c. Surface tension
   d. Viscosity

4. **Such Solutions Having Some Osmotic Pressures are termed**
   a. Isobaric
   b. Isochoric
   c. Isotopic
   d. Isotonic

5. **The Vapor Pressure of a Solution Containing a non-volatile Solute is directly Proportional to the.......**
   a. Osmotic pressure of the solute.
   b. Molarity of the solvent.
   c. Mole fraction of solvent.
   d. **Mole fraction of solute.**

Chapter - 2

Electrochemistry

Introduction

Electrochemistry

The branch of chemistry that deals with interconversion electricity (flow of electrons) and chemical reactions.

And the means chemical Reactions that involve transfer of electrons (reduction and oxidation).

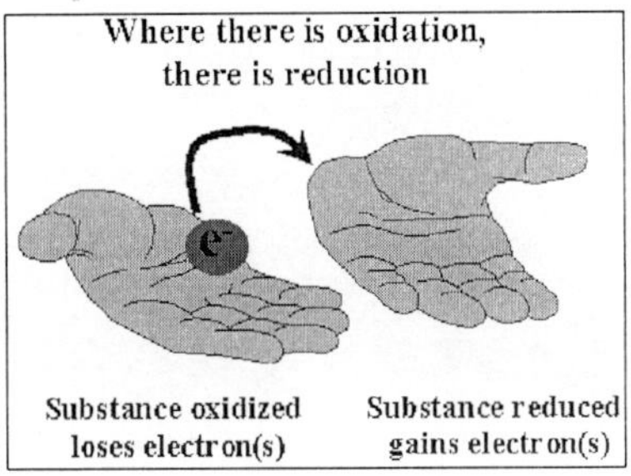

Source: www.bouman.chem.georgetown.edu

Electrochemical Cell

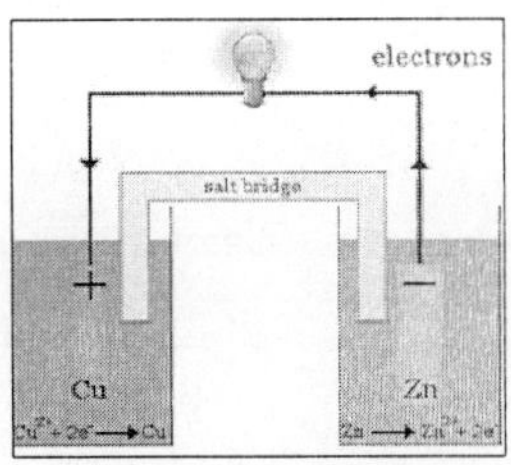

www.chemicol.com

A device which converts electrical energy

Into chemical energy is called as electro-

Chemical cell or voltaic cell or galvanic cell.

E.g. Daniel cell, dry cell.

Electrolytic Cell

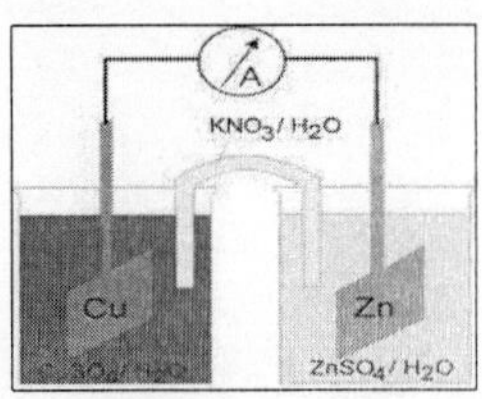

Source: www.differencebetween.net

A device which converts electrical energy into Chemical energy is called as electrolytic cell.

E.g. Electrolytic purification of copper.

(Electrolysis)

Terms Used in Electrochemistry

Cell

A device or an arrangement which converts chemical energy into electrical energy or electrical energy into chemical energy is called as a cell.

Battery

It is a combination of two or more cell arranged in series or parallel.

E.g. In 6-volt lead storage battery in which there is combination of three 2-volt cell connected in series.

www.electronics.howstuffworks.com

Cell Reaction

As cell is formed by combination of two electrodes, each electrode is half-cell or single electrode and the reaction takes place on half-cell is called as half-cell reaction.

The sum of half -cell reactions taking place on each electrode is called as net cell reaction.

On one electrode oxidation (loss of electron) takes place while at another electrode reduction (gain of electron) takes place.

The electrode on which oxidation takes place has negative potential.

The electrode on which reduction takes place has positive potential.

Reversible Cell

A cell which satisfy the condition of thermodynamic reversibility conditions is known as reversible cell.

1. That is they should have different driving and opposing force.
2. There should be possible to reverse the reaction by applying slightly greater force than acting force.
3. Daniel cell satisfy all the conditions.

$Zn^-/ZnSO_4$ (a=1)//$CuSO_4$ (a=1)/Cu^+

Irreversible Cell

A cell which do not satisfy the reversibility conditions is known as irreversible cell.

Zn^+/H_2SO_4 (a=1)/Cu^-

Electromotive Force and its Measurement

The difference of potential which causes flows of current between the two electrodes is known as electromotive force of a cell.

This is measured in Volt (V)

Measurement of EMF by Poggendorff compensation method

1. EMF is measured by voltmeter, however this has some drawbacks

- It draws current from a cell.
- Large current flows disturbs the equilibrium.
- When current drawn from cell, concentration of electrolyte changes.

2. Thus true EMF cannot be measured by voltmetre
3. Therefore accurate measurement of EMF is done by using potentiometer. It works on principle of Poggendorff compensation methods.
4. It is stated as 'The EMF of the cell is balanced by an equal and opposite EMF of a standard cell so that no current flows.'

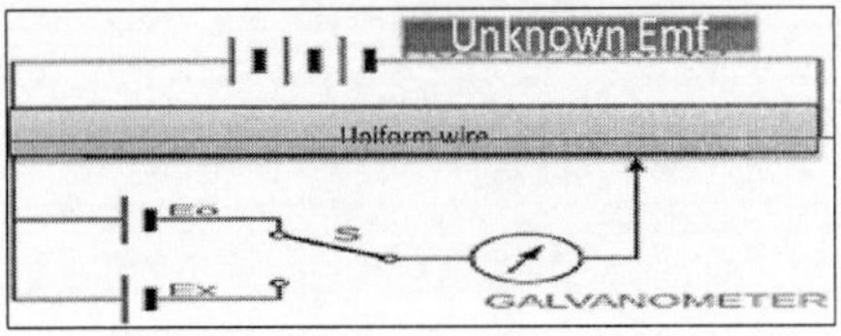

Source: www.de.m.wikipedia.org

1. First standard cell Eo is put in circuit and sliding contact is moved in such a way that galvanometer shows no deflection
2. The length AD is measured

3. The process is repeated with cell ex and new length AD' is measured.

4. The EMF of std. cell Eo and working cell Ex is related as-

$$\frac{Ex}{Eo} = \frac{AD}{AD'}$$

$$Ex = \frac{AD}{AD'} \times Eo$$

Thus by measuring AD, AD' and Eo, Ex (Unkown EMF) can be calculated.

Note-

- Es must be greater than ex.
- The galvanometer must be highly sensitive to experience even a small potential.

Standard Cell

The cell is standard when-

1. The potential of the cell is exactly known.
2. Potential must be reproducible and constant with time.
3. Cell should be reversible.
4. The standard cell have very low temperature co-efficient.
5. There should not be permanent damage of the cell due to passage of high current through it.

The Weston cell satisfies all these conditions therefore it is ''Weston standard''.

There are two types of Weston standard cell:-

Weston Standard Cell

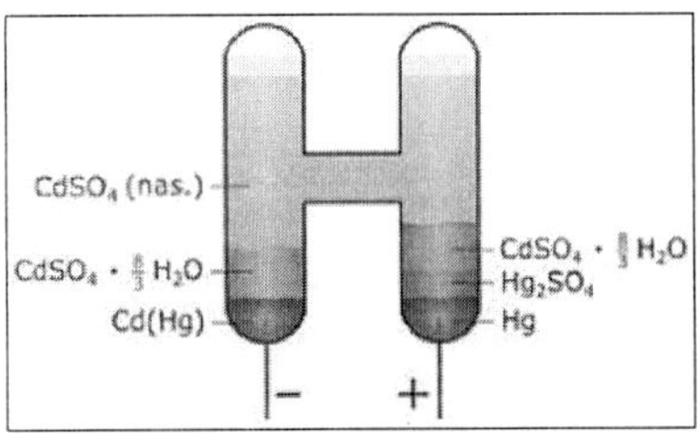

Source: www.it.wikipedia.org

The cell representation is-

$Cd(Hg)/CdSO_4 .8/3\ H_2O/CdSO_4\ (satd)/Hg(l), HgSO_4\ /Hg^+$

- It consist H shaped glass vessel in which platinum wire are attached at bottom of both the limbs.
- It left limb 12.5% Cd – amalgam as taken at base on which CdSO4 crystal is spread. This arm will act as negative electrode.
- In right limb, at base pure mercury is taken, covered with Hg_2SO4 in Hg paste and then sprinkled with CdSO4 crystal. This is now positive terminal.
- The entire vessel is filled with saturated CdSO4 soln.
- Both limb of H-Shaped vessel is sealed with wax at top.

The reversible reaction in Weston standard cell is-

$Cd\ (s) \rightarrow Cd^{+2} + 2e-$

$Cd^{+2} + SO_4^{-2} + 8/3\ H_2O \rightarrow CdSO_4.\ 8/3\ H_2O + 2e-$

The total reaction at –ve electrode-

$Cd^{+2} + SO_4^{-2} + 8/3\ H_2O \rightarrow CdSO_4.\ 8/3\ H_2O + 2e-$

At +ve electrode the recduction rection will takes place-

$HgSO_4\ (s) + 2e- \rightarrow 2Hg + SO_4^{-2}$

The net cell reaction is-

$Cd\ (s) + HgSO_4\ (s) + 8/3\ H_2O\ (l) \rightarrow CdSO_4.\ 8/3\ H_2O\ (s) + 2Hg\ (l)$

The potential of the cell at 20^0C is 1.01830 volts and at 25^0C it is 1.01807 volts.

Convention regarding sign of EMF:

The maximum electrical work is given by-

Wmax = nFE

Where n= number of electron involved in cell reaction

F = faradays constant of electricity

We know that maximum work is obtained by decrease in free energy (ΔG)

Therefore,

$\Delta G = -nFE$

-ve sign indicates that the free energy decreases with maximum work done.

Free energy of the reaction can be calculated by knowing EMF (E).

Table showing Sign of ΔG and EMF for reactions.

S. No.	Free Energy Change	EMF	Type of Reaction
1	- ve	+ve	Spontaneous
2	+ve	-ve	Non spontaneous
3	0	0	Equilibrium

Single Electrode Potential

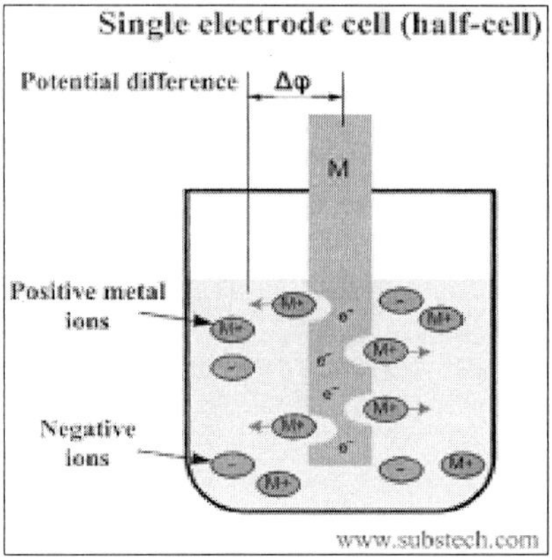

Source: http://www.qsstudy.com

Single Electrode Potential

The metal electrode contact with a solution containing its own ion is called a half cell or single electrode.

E.g., Cu-Electrode

The copper electrode dipped in its own ion solution (Cu^{++} ion) forms half-cell or single electrode.

E.g. Daniel Cell

Here, Zinc electrode dipped in its own solution Zn^{++} form one half-cell or single electrode. And copper electrode dipped in its own ion solution Cu^{++} forms another half-cell or single electrode. Both half-cell combines and form complete cell.

The oxidation and reduction take place at the electrode depends on to which electrode coupled.

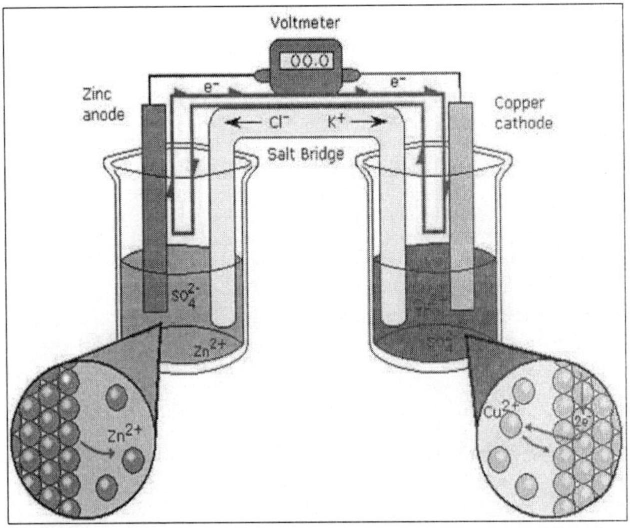

Source: www.askiitians.com

Daniel cell.

Standard Electrode Potential at 25^{0}c for Reduction Reactions

TABLE 18.1 Standard Reduction Potentials at 25°C

	Reduction Half-Reaction		E° (V)	
Stronger oxidizing agent	$F_2(g) + 2e^-$	$\longrightarrow 2F^-(aq)$	2.87	Weaker reducing agent
	$H_2O_2(aq) + 2H^+(aq) + 2e^-$	$\longrightarrow 2H_2O(l)$	1.78	
	$MnO_4^-(aq) + 8H^+(aq) + 5e^-$	$\longrightarrow Mn^{2+}(aq) + 4H_2O(l)$	1.51	
	$Cl_2(g) + 2e^-$	$\longrightarrow 2Cl^-(aq)$	1.36	
	$Cr_2O_7^{2-}(aq) + 14H^+(aq) + 6e^-$	$\longrightarrow 2Cr^{3+}(aq) + 7H_2O(l)$	1.33	
	$O_2(g) + 4H^+(aq) + 4e^-$	$\longrightarrow 2H_2O(l)$	1.23	
	$Br_2(l) + 2e^-$	$\longrightarrow 2Br^-(aq)$	1.09	
	$Ag^+(aq) + e^-$	$\longrightarrow Ag(s)$	0.80	
	$Fe^{3+}(aq) + e^-$	$\longrightarrow Fe^{2+}(aq)$	0.77	
	$O_2(g) + 2H^+(aq) + 2e^-$	$\longrightarrow H_2O_2(aq)$	0.70	
	$I_2(s) + 2e^-$	$\longrightarrow 2I^-(aq)$	0.54	
	$O_2(g) + 2H_2O(l) + 4e^-$	$\longrightarrow 4OH^-(aq)$	0.40	
	$Cu^{2+}(aq) + 2e^-$	$\longrightarrow Cu(s)$	0.34	
	$Sn^{4+}(aq) + 2e^-$	$\longrightarrow Sn^{2+}(aq)$	0.15	
	$2H^+(aq) + 2e^-$	$\longrightarrow H_2(g)$	0	
	$Pb^{2+}(aq) + 2e^-$	$\longrightarrow Pb(s)$	−0.13	
	$Ni^{2+}(aq) + 2e^-$	$\longrightarrow Ni(s)$	−0.26	
	$Cd^{2+}(aq) + 2e^-$	$\longrightarrow Cd(s)$	−0.40	
	$Fe^{2+}(aq) + 2e^-$	$\longrightarrow Fe(s)$	−0.45	
	$Zn^{2+}(aq) + 2e^-$	$\longrightarrow Zn(s)$	−0.76	
	$2H_2O(l) + 2e^-$	$\longrightarrow H_2(g) + 2OH^-(aq)$	−0.83	
	$Al^{3+}(aq) + 3e^-$	$\longrightarrow Al(s)$	−1.66	
	$Mg^{2+}(aq) + 2e^-$	$\longrightarrow Mg(s)$	−2.37	
	$Na^+(aq) + e^-$	$\longrightarrow Na(s)$	−2.71	
Weaker oxidizing agent	$Li^+(aq) + e^-$	$\longrightarrow Li(s)$	−3.04	Stronger reducing agent

Source: www.quora.com

Reference Electrodes

- Primary reference electrode -
- Standard Hydrogen electrode-

It is primary reference electrode whose potential is fixed at zero volt at 25^0C

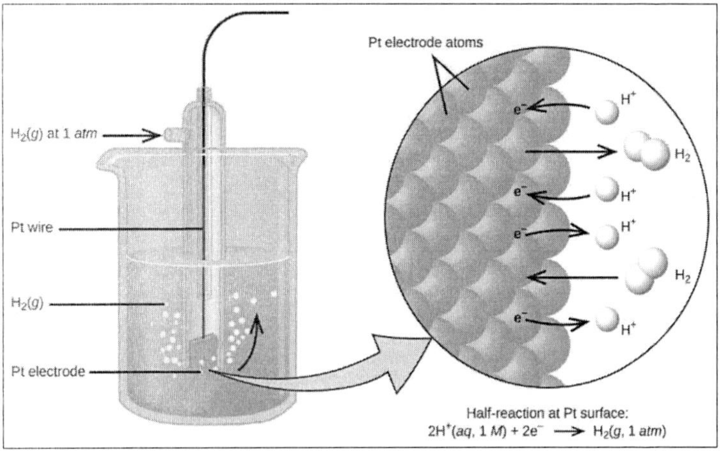

Source: https://chem.libretexts.org/

Construction

- A small inner glass tube contains small quantity of mercury.
- A platinum wire connected with platinum piece sealed with small glass tube.
- This electrode covered with outer jacket having inlet for H_2 has.
- This electrode consist small platinum piece coated with platinum black it acts as a catalyst.
- The glass jacket has number of holes at base.
- The electrode is then placed in HCl Solution of 1M concentration

Working

- Pure H_2 gas is bubbled slowly through inlet at 1 atm pressure on the surface of Pt-sheet
- H_2 gas adsorbed on this Pt-sheet.
- An equilibrium is rapidly established on the surface of platinum foil.

- That is adsorbed Hydrogen gas dissociates into H+ ions on Pt surface.

Therefore Reaction is,

$$\frac{1}{2} H (g) \rightleftharpoons 2H^{+} + e^{-}$$

The potential of hydrogen electrode is 0.00 volt at $20^{0}C$.

Advantages

- It is used at any P^{H}.
- Efficiency is cannot affected by salts.
- Its potential is taken as zero.

Limitations

- Difficult to maintain 1atm pressure.
- Difficult to maintain H+ ion concentration.
- Impurities of H2 gas can make electrode inactive and irreversible.

Calomel Electrodes

Secondary Reference Electrode

- The potential of the electrodes when determined with respect to SHE then it is called as secondary reference electrode.
- Saturated calomel electrode used as reference electrode' its potential is -2.042 V.
- Representation-

  Hg/HgCl2 (s), KCl (aq).

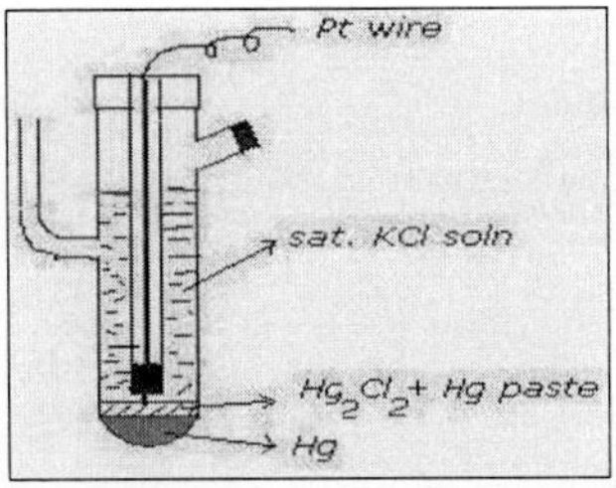

Source: http://mgvsatya.blogspot.com

- It consists of glass tube, having side bent arm.
- A small quantity of pure mercury is placed at bottom of glass tube.
- It is then covered with paste of Hg_2Cl_2 mercurous chloride in pure Hg.

- The base of tube and bent arm is filled with mercury and the platinum wire sealed at the bottom of tube for connection.
- Entire tube and side arm is filled up with appropriate (saturated/0.1N/1N) KCl solution.

Working

- The platinum wire carries electrical charges.
- The calomel electrode is represented by,

$Hg/HgCl_2$ (s) (Saturated), KCl (Solution)

The reduction reaction is-

$\frac{1}{2} HgCl_2 (s) + e^- \rightarrow Hg (l) + Cl^-$

The potential of electrode is depends on concentration of KCl solution at each temperature which is shown in table-

Electrode	Representation	E_{red} 25^0C/Volt	EMF (At Temperature 25^0C)
0.1 N Calomel	$Hg/HgCl_2$ (s), KCl (0.1N)	0.3338	$0.3338 - 7x10^{-4}$
1N calomel	$Hg/HgCl_2$ (s), KCl (1N)	0.280	$0.280 - 2.4 x10^{-4}$
Saturated calomel	$Hg/HgCl_2$ (s), KCl (Satd.)	0.2415	$0.2415 - 7.6 x 10^{-4}$

Advantages

- It is easy to set up.
- The results is highly reproducible.

Thermodynamics and EMF.

1. **Free Energy Change (ΔG)**

The energy available for doing useful work is called as Free energy.

The relation between the EMF and Free energy change is given as-

$$\Delta G = -nFE$$

Where, n = number of electrons involved during cell reaction.

F= faraday's constant =96500 coloumbs.

2. **Enthalpy Change (ΔH)**

The Gibbs- Helmholtz equation is given as,

$\Delta G = \Delta H + T (d \Delta G/dT) p$

Where, ΔG= free energy change

ΔH = enthalpy change

T= Temperature in Kelvin

And, T (d ΔG/dT) p is variation in free energy change with temperature.

Consider the equation,

$$\Delta G = -nFE$$

By differentiating this equation w.r.t temperature

$$(d\ \Delta G/dT)_p = -nF\ (dE/dt)_p$$

Substituting ΔG and $(d\ \Delta G/dT)_p$ in above equation.

$$-nfE = \Delta H + T\ [-nF\ (dE/dt)_p]$$

Rearranging above equation,

$$\Delta H = nF\ [T\ (dE/dt)_p - E]$$

(dE/dT) p is known as temperature co-efficient of the cell.

Definition

Temperature co-efficient is defined as variation of EMF of the cell with temperature. It is expressed in volts per 0^0K unit.

Entropy Change- (ΔS)

The relation between enthalpy change ΔH and free energy change ΔG is given as,

$$\Delta G = \Delta H - T\Delta S$$

$$\Delta H = \Delta G + T\Delta S \qquad \ldots 1$$

Where, ΔS = entropy change at temperature T^0 K.

Enthalpy is given by,

$$\Delta H = nF\ [T\ (dE/dT)_P - E]$$

We know,

$$\Delta G = -nFE$$

Substituting ΔG and ΔH,

Equation-1 becomes,

$$nF\ [T\ (dE/dT)_P - E] = -nFE + T\Delta S$$

Dividing throughout by Nf

$$T\ (dE/dt)_P = T\ \Delta S/nF$$

Rearranging the equation we get,

$\Delta S = nF\,(dE/dt)_P$

Above equation is used to calculate entropy change of a reaction by knowing temperature co-efficient of EMF.

Nernst Equation

This equation gives the relation between electrode potential and cell EMF as a function of initial and final activities of substances involved in cell reaction.

Consider general reaction,

$aA + Bb + \ldots\ldots\ldots = Cc + dD$

The change in free energy ΔG as a function of activities of reactants and product respectively.

$$\Delta G = \Delta^0 G + RT\ln \frac{(a_C{}^c \times a_D{}^d \ldots.)}{(a_A{}^a \times a_B{}^b \ldots..)}$$

Where Δ^0G is standard free energy, T is absolute temperature K^0 and R is molar gas constant.

a_c, a_d ....are activities of products,

a_a, a_b ....are activities of reactants.

Also we know,

$\Delta G = -nFE$

And $\Delta^0 G = -nFE^0$

$-nFE = -nFE^0 + RT\ln (a_C{}^c \times a_D{}^d \ldots)/ (a_A{}^a \times a_B{}^b \ldots)$

Divide through -out by –nF

$E = E^0 - RT/nF \ln (a_C{}^c \times a_D{}^d \ldots.)/ (a_A{}^a \times a_B{}^b \ldots..)$

$E = E^0 - 2.303\ RT/nF \log_{10} (a_C{}^c \times a_D{}^d \ldots)/(a_A{}^a \times a_B{}^b \ldots)$ ...1

Above equation is used to calculate electrode potential or cell potential.

When activities of reactants and products are unity, then the EMF of the cell/electrode is equal to its standard potential.

$E=E^0$

At 25^0C (298^0K)

R= 8.314 Joules

F = 96487 coloumb

$$2.303 \frac{RT}{F} = \frac{2.303 \times 8.314 \times 298}{96487}$$

Therefore,

$$E = E^0 - \frac{0.0591}{n} \log_{10} \frac{(a_C^c \times a_D^d \ldots)}{(a_A^a \times a_B^b \ldots)} \quad \ldots\ldots\ldots 2$$

Equation 1 & 2 are Nernst equation used to calculate EMF of electrode or cell.

Numerical Problems

I) Determination of Standard Cell/Electrode Potential

Standard electrode potential is the cell potential under standard state conditions that is at concentrations of 1 mole per liter (1 M) and pressures of 1 atmosphere at 25°C.

To calculate the standard cell potential for a reaction-

- First write the oxidation and reduction half-reactions for the cell.
- Note the reduction potential, ($E^o_{reduction}$), for the reduction half-reaction in a electrochemical series of reduction potentials.
- Then note the reduction potential for the oxidation half-cell reaction and reverse the sign to obtain the standard oxidation potential.

For the oxidation half-reaction, $E^o_{oxidation} = - E^o_{reduction}$.

- Add the reduction potentials and oxidation potential of the half cells to get the total standard cell potential by using below given equation-

$$\mathbf{E^o_{cell} = E^o_{reduction} + E^o_{oxidation}}$$

Example-1

Find the standard cell potential for an electrochemical cell with the following cell reaction.

$$\mathbf{Zn(s) + Cu^{2+}(aq) \rightarrow Zn^{2+}(aq) + Cu(s)}$$

Solution

Write the each of the half-reactions.

For Oxidation process $\quad Zn(s) \rightarrow Zn^{2+}(aq) + 2\ e^-$

For Reduction process $Cu^{2+}(aq) + 2e^- \rightarrow Cu(s)$

Note the standard potentials for the reduction half-cell reaction.

$$E^o_{\text{reduction of }Cu2+} = +0.339\ V$$

Then note the standard reduction potential for the oxidation reaction and change the sign.

$$E^o_{\text{reduction of }Zn2+} = -0.762\ V$$

$$E^o_{\text{oxidation of }Zn} = -(-0.762\ V) = +0.762\ V$$

Add the half-cell potentials together to get the total standard cell potential.

Oxidation Process:	**$Zn(s) \rightarrow Zn^{2+}(aq) + 2e^-$**	**$E^o_{ox.} = -E^o_{red.} = -(-0.762\ V) = +0.762\ V$**
Reduction Process:	$Cu^{2+}(aq) + 2e^- \rightarrow Cu(s)$	$E^o_{red.} = +0.339\ V$
Total:	$Zn(s) + Cu^{2+}(aq) \rightarrow Zn^{2+}(aq) + Cu(s)$	$E^o_{cell} = +1.101\ V$

II) Determining Non-Standard Electrode/Cell Potentials

To determine the cell/electrode potential when the conditions are other than standard state (that is when, concentrations is not 1 molar and/or pressures not 1 atmosphere):

- Determine the standard state cell potential.
- Determine the non-standard cell /electrode potential using Nernst equation by knowing-
- Value for Q, the reaction quotient.
- Value for n, the number of electrons involved in the reaction.

$E_{cell} = E^0_{cell} - 2.303\ RT/nF\ \log_{10} \underline{(a_C{}^c \times a_D{}^d....)}/ (a_A{}^a \times a_B{}^b.....)$

$E_{cell} = E^o_{cell} - 2.303\ RT/nF\ \ln Q$

Where, $Q = \underline{(a_C{}^c \times a_D{}^d....)}/ (a_A{}^a \times a_B{}^b.....)$

E_{cell} = cell potential at non-standard state conditions

E^o_{cell} = standard state cell potential

R = constant (8.31 J/mole K)

T = absolute temperature (Kelvin scale)

F = Faraday's constant (96,485 C/mole e^-)

n = number of moles of electrons involved in the reaction occurring in the cell.

Considering temperature of the cell remains at 25°C, the equation will become:

$$E_{cell} = E^{o}_{cell} - (0.0591/n) \log_{10} Q$$

Example-2

Predict the cell potential for the following reaction when the pressure of the oxygen gas is 2.50 atm, the hydrogen ion concentration is 0.10 M, and the bromide ion concentration is 0.25 M.

$$\mathbf{O_2 (g) + 4\ H^+ (aq) + 4\ Br^- (aq) \rightarrow 2\ H_2O\ (l) + 2\ Br_2\ (l)}$$

Solution

- Calculate the standard cell potential for the reaction, E^{o}_{cell}, using values given in electrochemical series.

Oxidation Process:	**$4\ Br^-(aq) \rightarrow 2\ Br_2(l) + 4\ e^-$**	**$E^{o}_{ox.} = - E^{o}_{red.} = - (+ 1.077\ V) = - 1.077\ V$**
Reduction process:	$O_2(g) + 4\ H^+(aq) + 4\ e- \rightarrow 2\ H_2O(l)$	$E^{o}_{red.} = + 1.229\ V$
Net cell reaction:	$O_2(g) + 4\ H^+(aq) + 4\ Br^-(aq) \rightarrow 2\ H_2O(l) + 2\ Br_2(l)$	$E^{o}_{cell} = + 0.152\ V$

Determine the new cell potential in non- standard state.

- Calculate the value for the reaction quotient, Q. (Note: We calculate Q using molar concentrations/ activities for solutions (for gases it is in pressure terms). Water and bromine are both liquids, therefore they are not included in the calculation of Q.)

$$Q = \frac{1}{P_{O2}\,[H^+]^4[Br^-]^4}$$

$$Q = \frac{1}{(2.50\ atm)(0.10\ M)^4(0.25\ M)^4}$$

$$Q = 1.02 \times 10^6$$

- Calculate the number of electrons which is involve in the balanced equation,

$$n = 4 \text{ moles of electrons}$$

- Substitute all the determined values into the Nernst equation

$$E_{cell} = + 0.152\ V - (0.0591/4) \log_{10} (1.02 \times 10^6)$$

$$E_{cell} = 0.063\ V$$

Classification of Electrodes

Electrode are classify in five types

1. **Metal-Metal Ion Electrode**

The metal rod dipped into its own ion solution forms this types of electrodes-

The general reaction is-

$M = M^{n+} + e-$

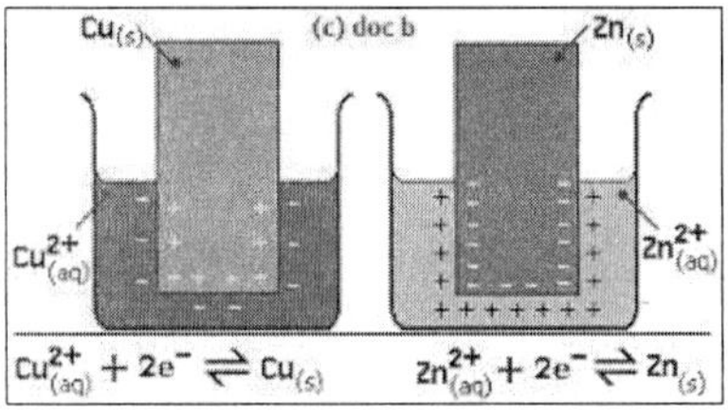

Source: http://www.docbrown.info

Applying Nernst equation-

$Em = E^0m - RT/nF\_ln\ a_{mn+}$

2. **Amalgam Electrode**

- The electrode consist of active metal in the form of amalgam dipping in metal ion.
- The electrical contact is mad by using inert metal such as pt

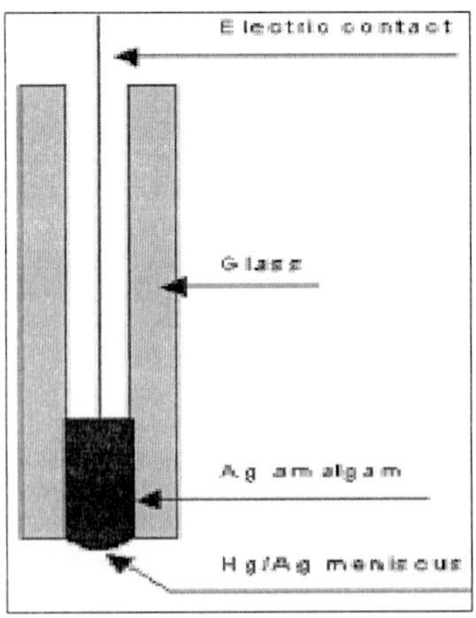

Source: https://www.researchgate.net

Eg, Pb (Hg)/ pb $^{2+}$ (a)

3. Gas Electrodes

It set up by bubbling gas about an inert metal wire or foil immersed in solution of ion to which the gas is reversible. The inert metal ion is usually platinum wire.

The gas electrode are SHE, chlorine electrode etc.

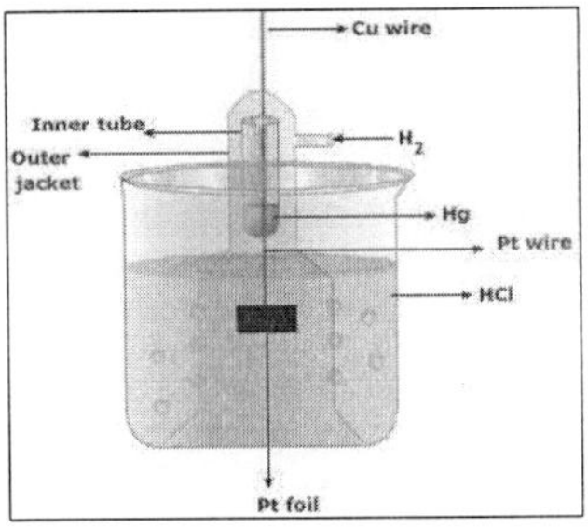

Source: http://giantwheels.blogspot.com

1. H2 Electrode

Pt/H2 (g) (P_{H2})/H+

$\frac{1}{2} H_2 = H^+ + e^-$

Therefore,

$E = E^0 - (RT/F) \ln (a_{H+}/P_{H2}^{1/2})$

4. Metal-Metal Insoluble Salt Electrode

The electrode of this type consist of a metal rod with one of its sparingly soluble salt and s solution containing the ion present in the salt other than the metal.

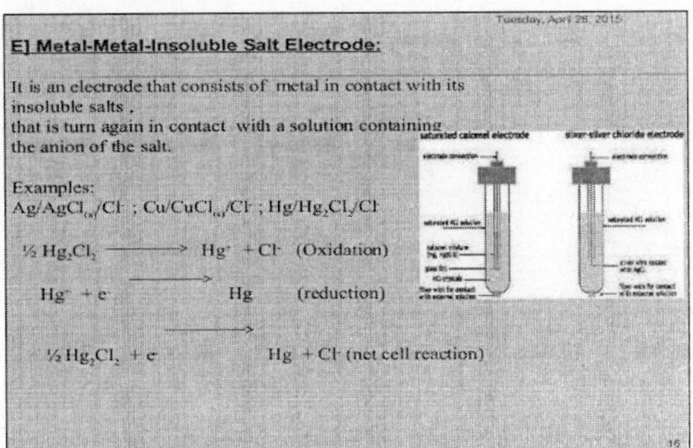

Source: www.slideshare.net

5. **Oxidation Reduction Electrodes**

In this electrode, EMF results due to presence of ions of a substance in two different oxidation states. Eg. When platinum wire is dipped in the solution of Fe^{+2} and Fe^{+3} ions both, it is found that potential is developed.

Reaction,

$Fe^{+3} + e^- = Fe^{+2}$

The EMF is given by,

E redox = E^0 redox – RT/nF_ln (a1/a2)

Multiple Choice Questions Practice

1. **Li Occupies Higher Position in the Electrochemical Series of Metals as Compared to Cu Since.**

   a) **The standard reduction potential of Li^+/Li is lower than that of Cu^{2+}/Cu**

   b) The standard reduction potential of Cu^{2+}/Cu is lower than that of Li^+/Li

   c) The standard oxidation potential of Li/Li^+ is lower than that of Cu/Cu^{2+}

   d) Li is smaller in size as compared to Cu.

2. **Which of the Following Element Act as Inert Electrode?**

   a) Cu

   b) Ag

   c) **Pt**

   d) None

3. **Stronger the Oxidizing Agent Greater is the……**

   a) Oxidation potential

   b) **Reduction potential**

   c) Redox potential

   d) EMF of cell

4. **In an Electrolytic Cell Current Flows?**

   a) From cathode to anode in outer circuit

   b) **From anode to cathode outside the cell**

   c) From cathode to anode inside the cell

   d) both b & c

5. **In a Galvanic Cell**

   a) **Chemical energy is converted into electricity.**
   b) Chemical energy is converted into heat.
   c) Electrical energy is converted into chemical energy.
   d) Electrical energy is converted into heat.

6. **For the Measurement of Standard Electrode Potential Zn is Dipped in**

   a) 1M ZnO solution
   b) **1M ZnSO4 solution**
   c) 1.5M ZnSO4 solution
   d) 1.6 MZnSO4 solution

7. **Zn(s)/Zn+2(aq) 1M || Cu+2(aq) 1M/Cu(s) is Representation of Reaction in**

   a) Daniel cell
   b) Downs cell
   c) **Voltaic cell**
   d) Nelsons cell

8. **H2 Gas in SHE is Filled at Pressure of**

   a) **298K**
   b) 300K
   c) 30K
   d) 310K

9. **Greater Value of Standard Reduction Potential Greater Will be Tendency.**

   a) To get oxidized
   b) To get reduced
   c) To accept electrons
   d) **Both b and c**

10. **Voltaic Cell is a**

    a) irreversible cell
    b) reversible cell
    c) alkaline cell
    d) All of the above.

Chapter - 3

Chemistry of Lanthanides Elements

Introduction

- The element in which the successive filing of e-s in n-2 f orbital is called f-block elements.
- There are 2 series 4f and 5f series and are called as Lanthanides series and actinides series. Resp.
- Lanthanum (57) is not a Lanthanides
- The series of 14 elements from Ce to Lu (58-71) are Lanthanides.

General Electronic Configuration of First Series of Lanthanides

Element	Symbol	Atomic Number	Expected electronic configuration	Observed electronic configuration
Lanthanum	La	57	[Xe] $4f^0\ 5d^1\ 6s^2$	[Xe] $4f^0\ 5d^1\ 6s^2$
Cerium	Ce	58	[Xe] $4f^1\ 5d^1\ 6s^2$	[Xe] $4f^2\ 5d^0\ 6s^2$
Praseodymium	Pr	59	[Xe] $4f^2\ 5d^1\ 6s^2$	[Xe] $4f^3\ 5d^0\ 6s^2$
Neodymium	Nd	60	[Xe] $4f^3\ 5d^1\ 6s^2$	[Xe] $4f^4\ 5d^0\ 6s^2$
Promethium	Pm	61	[Xe] $4f^4\ 5d^1\ 6s^2$	[Xe] $4f^5\ 5d^0\ 6s^2$
Samarium	Sm	62	[Xe] $4f^5\ 5d^1\ 6s^2$	[Xe] $4f^6\ 5d^0\ 6s^2$
Europium	Eu	63	[Xe] $4f^6\ 5d^1\ 6s^2$	[Xe] $4f^7\ 5d^0\ 6s^2$
Gadolinium	Gd	64	[Xe] $4f^7\ 5d^1\ 6s^2$	[Xe] $4f^7\ 5d^1\ 6s^2$
Terbium	Tb	65	[Xe] $4f^8\ 5d^1\ 6s^2$	[Xe] $4f^9\ 5d^0\ 6s^2$
Dysprosium	Dy	66	[Xe] $4f^9\ 5d^1\ 6s^2$	[Xe] $4f^{10}\ 5d^0\ 6s^2$
Holmium	Ho	67	[Xe] $4f^{10}\ 5d^1\ 6s^2$	[Xe] $4f^{11}\ 5d^0\ 6s^2$
Erbium	Er	68	[Xe] $4f^{11}\ 5d^1\ 6s^2$	[Xe] $4f^{12}\ 5d^0\ 6s^2$
Thulium	Tm	69	[Xe] $4f^{12}\ 5d^1\ 6s^2$	[Xe] $4f^{13}\ 5d^0\ 6s^2$
Ytterbium	Yb	70	[Xe] $4f^{13}\ 5d^1\ 6s^2$	[Xe] $4f^{14}\ 5d^0\ 6s^2$
Lutetium	Lu	71	[Xe] $4f^{14}\ 5d^1\ 6s^2$	[Xe] $4f^{14}\ 5d^1\ 6s^2$

The General -E.C is-

$$[Xe],\ n\text{-}2\ f^{(1\text{-}14)},\ (n\text{-}1)\ d^{1 or 0},\ nS^2$$

- The next electrons are enter in inner (n-2) 4f shell from Ce to Lu
- In most of elements electrons move from 5d orbital to 4f level.
- This is due to increase in the stability of 4f shell.
- Lu has $5d^1$ due to completely filled 4f shell.
- All these element are similar in chemical properties.

Oxidation States

- +3 is the most common O.S in Lanthanides.
- Some of these also shows +2 and +4 O.S
- The elements la, Gd, and Lu show +3 state due to extra stability of 4f empty, half-filled and completely filled.
- The elements which shows +2 and +4 state due to stable state of f0, f7 and f14.

Oxidation state

- Common oxidation state is +3 more stable.
- Loses of two 6s electron and one 5d or 4f electron.
- Some either show +2 or +4 Oxidation state.
- Ln [Xe] $4f^0$ $5d^1$ $6s^2$ and Ln+3 [Xe]$4f^0$ $5d^0$ $6s^0$

Ln, Pm, Ho, Eb, Lu	+3
Ce, Pr, Tb, Dy	+3, +4
Sm, Eu, Tm, Yb	+2, +3
Nd,	+2, +3, +3

Extraction and Uses

1. **Occurrence**

The mineral containing lanthanides elements are-

a. **Monazite sand-**

- It is most important and widely used mineral of Lanthanides.
- It is mixture of lanthanide phosphate, trivalent phosphate of lower Lanthanides, small amount of yttrium (Y) and higher Lanthanides.

b. **Bastnaesite-**

- It is the mixed fluorocarbonate of Lanthanides.

c. **Xenotime**

- It is an orthophosphate of Y–earths.

Extraction of Lanthanides from Monazite Ore

Monazite is the most important mineral of Lanthanides, it contain Ln-Phosphates 88%, and Th-phosphates 12% along with small amount of Zr, Fe and Ti in the form of silicate.

Extraction Process-(See Flow Chart)

1. Ore is digested with conc. H_2SO_4 at 200^0C to form paste of sulphates.

2. Then sulphates is seperated by centrifugation and wash with cold water.
3. Zr, Ti, and Fe are being insoluble in cold water, therefore they get seperated.
4. Thorium remain in solution which removed as insoluble phosphates.
5. The solution now only contain sulphates of lanthanides, which treated with Na_2SO_4, the lighter Ln's precipitates as double sulphates while the higher Ln's remain in solution.
6. The ppt of double phosphates are treated with hot NaOH to form mixture of oxides and hydroxides.
7. The mixture is wash and dried at 100°C, where Ce is oxidised to CeO_2 and seperated out.

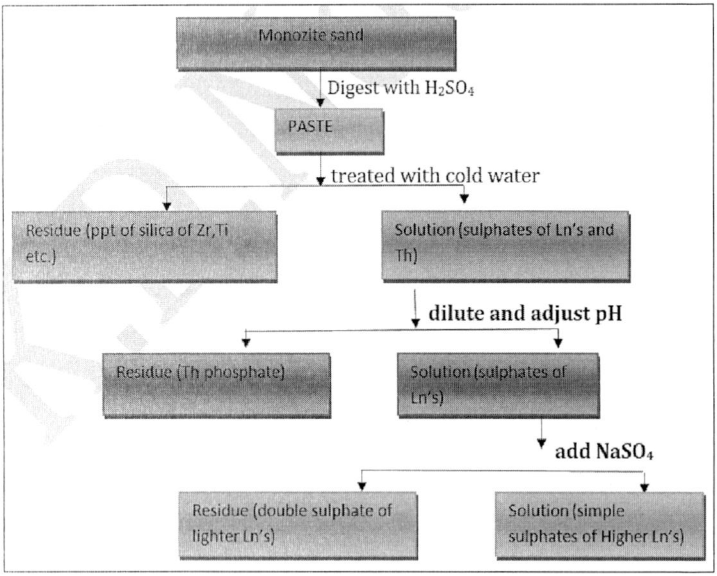

Flow Chart for Extraction Proces

Uses of Lanthanides

1. Mixture of la and Ln's is called misch metal. It is mixture of Ce (50%), La (40%), Fe (7%) and other (3%). misch metal is added to steel for strength.
2. Misch metal is also used in lighter flints. It is used in LPG stove lighter, cigarette lighter to produce bullets.

3. La_2O_3 is used in crooks lens which protect from U.V rays.
4. $CeSO_4$ is used as oxidizing agent in volumetric analysis.
5. Ln's oxides are used in colour TV's.
6. Ce-salts are used in dying cotton as well and medicines.

Separation of Lanthanides Elements-

All lanthanides are similar size therefore there separation is very difficult.

The methods for separations are as follows-

1. **Solvent Extraction Methods**
   a. This separation is based on different in distribution coefficient of Ln's salts between salts and immiscible organic solvents.
   b. In Craig counter apparatus, aqueous solution of Ln's salts is shake with organic solvents tri-n-butyl phosphates and get extracted.
   c. By these methods 95% Gd is obtained.
2. **Ion Exchange Chromatography Methods-(See Image 3)**
   a. This is column chromatography method in which cation exchange resin is used.
   b. The tendency of Ln's cation to replace H+ ion on cation exchange resin increases with increase in cation size.
   c. Ln's having largest size (La+3) is held strongly while ion with smallest size (Lu+3) is held less strongly.

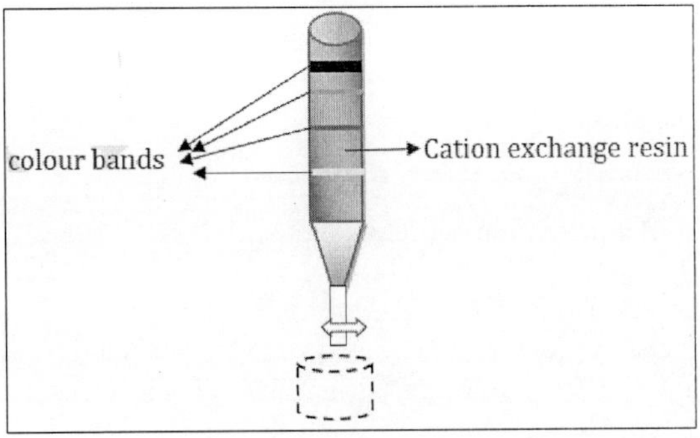

Lanthanides Contractions

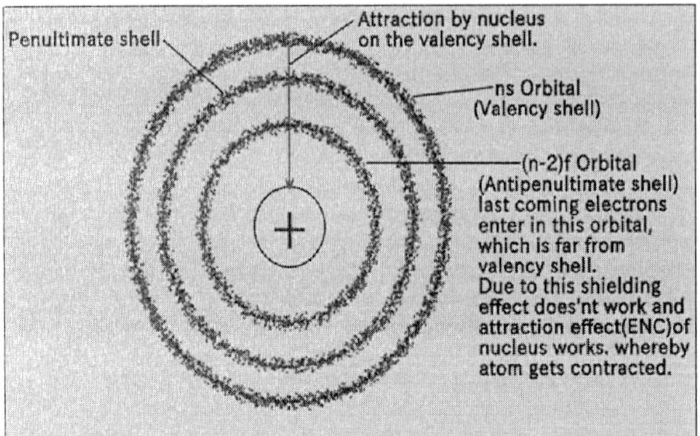

Contraction in f-block elements.

Defination- "the decrease in atomic size and ionic radii with increase in atomic number from Ce to Lu, is called lanthanides contraction."

- In general, in a period from left to right, the atomic and ionic radii decreases, because of the presence of extra e-s in an orbital which shields (defence) the extra nuclear charge.
- These electrons get pull closer towards nucleus.
- These shielding effects of electrons decrease the size of atoms.
- The shielding effect is in order of S> P>D>F.
- The f- orbital has poor shielding effect.
- With increase in atomic number, there is also increase in a nuclear charge hence 4f electrons provides poor shielding, therefore valence shell shrinks inwards.
- Hence atomic size decreases.

Effects of Lanthanides Contractions

Due to the Lanthanides contraction-

1. The electropositive nature, ionic radius, metallic characters and basicity of hydroxides decreases due to Lanthanides contractions. Hence Lu is least metallic among Lanthanides.
2. The hardness, Melting point and Boiling point of these entire elements increase from Ce to Lu due to increase in contraction of atomic size.
3. The Ionization energy, the electro negativity and the standard electrodes potential increases from Ce to Lu.

4. Due to Lanthanides contractions the ionic radii and chemical properties of Y, Dy and Ho are almost identical. Therefore it is difficult to separate.

Effect of Lanthanides Contractions on Post Lanthanides

- The elements which follow the lanthanides are post Lanthanides.
- Due to lanthanides contractions the properties of the elements of 2nd and 3rd transitions series are more similar than the 1st and 2nd series elements.
- Hence the pairs of Zr and Hf, Nb and Ta, Mo and W Posses almost same size.
- Hence they have same chemical properties, and this pairs of elements are called chemical twins.

First Series Elements	Sc	Ti	V	Cr	Mn	Fe	Co	Ni	Cu	Zn
Atomic radii (pm)	144	132	122	117	117	117	116	115	117	125
Second Series Elements	Y	Zr	Nb	Mo	Tc	Ru	Rh	Pd	Ag	Cd
Atomic radii (pm)	180	160	160	146	136	134	134	137	144	154
Third Series Elements	La	Hf	Ta	W	Re	Os	Ir	Pt	Au	Hg
Atomic radii (pm)	187	159	146	139	137	135	136	138	144	157

Chapter - 4

Chemistry of Actinoids Elements

Introduction

- The series of 14 elements ~~in~~ from Th 90 – Lr 103 in which 5f orbital are successively filled, are called as actinides or actinons.
- The actinides series start from Ac 89, Th 90 U 92 to the artificial prepared synthetic elements called as transuranic elements.

Elements	Symbol	Electronic configuration
Thorium	Th	$6d^2\ 7s^2$
Protactinium	Pa	$5f^2\ 6d^1\ 7s^2$
Uranium	U	$5f^3\ 6d^1\ 7s^2$
Neptunium	Np	$5f^4\ 6d^1\ 7s^2$
Plutonium	Pu	$5f^6\ 7s^2$
Americium	Am	$5f^7\ 7s^2$
Curium	Cm	$5f^7\ 6d^1\ 7s^2$
Berkelium	Bk	$5f^9\ 7s^2$
Californium	Cf	$5f^{10}\ 7s^2$
Einstenium	Es	$5f^{11}\ 7s^2$
Fermium	Fm	$5f^{12}\ 7s^2$
Mendelevium	Md	$5f^{13}\ 7s^2$
Nobelium	No	$5f^{14}\ 7s^2$
Lawrencium	Lr	$5f^{14}\ 6d^1\ 7s^2$

Image - 6

The Electronic Structure

(See Image-6)

In these elements the electrons are added to the antipenultimate shell 5f keeping 6th and 7th shell incompletely filled and completely filled respectively.

- These are also called as inner transitions elements.
- The general eletronic configuration.

$$[Rn]_{86},\ 5f^{0-14},\ 6d^{0-1}, 7S^2.$$

The Position of Actinides in Periodic Table

They belongs to 3rd group of 7th periods of periodic table.

- Actually they stops the 4th transition series of d-block in 7th periods
- There actual position is in between Ac (89) and Rf (104).

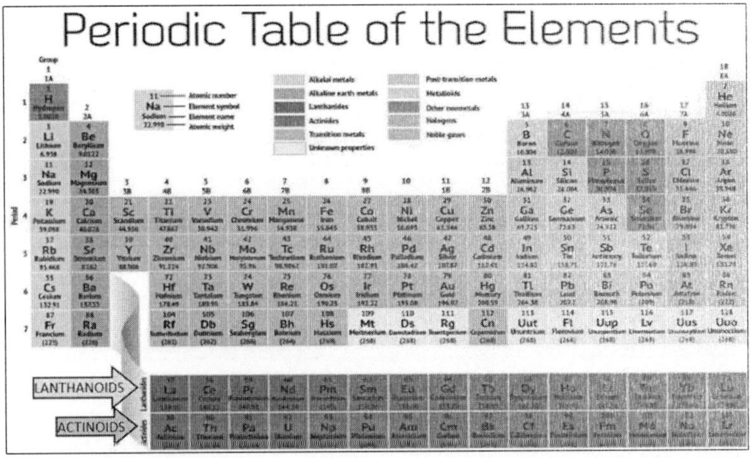

Oxidation States

The most common O.S is +3

- They also shows +2 to +7 O.S.
- The +2 O.S is rare.
- Am+2 and No+2 states is stable due to f7 and f14 configuration.
- The +4 O.S is stable for Th, Pu.
- The +5 O.S stable for Pa, Np.
- The +6 O.S is stable for U, Np,Pu and Am.

Ac	Th	Pa	U	Np	Pu	Am	Cm	Bk	Cf	Es	Fm	Md	No	Lr
						(2)			(2)	(2)	2	2	2	-
3	(3)	(3)	3	3	3	3	3	3	3	3	3	3	3	3
	4	4	4	4	4	4	4	4	(4)					
		5	5	5	5	5								
			6	6	6	6								
				(7)	7									

Occurrence of Actinides

Th and U are naturally occuring elements

- While others are prepared synthetically by nuclear reactions
- Hence these elements having atomic number higher than U are called transuranic elements

- The most important ore of thorium is monozite sand.
- Another ore of actinides is thiorite (ThO2), pitch blende (UO2).

Preparation of Actinides

The elements having higher atomic number than uranium (U-92) have been prepared by various types of nuclear reactions are called as transuranic/ man made elements.

The elements from Np 93 to Lr 103 are prepared by following methods-

1. **Neutron Bombardments Methods**

- This process is carried out in nuclear reactor in which neutrons collides with the atomic nuclei to forms nuclide with large mass to charge ratio.
- The process of synthesis of transuranic elements involves bombardment of neutrons to produce nuclides that becomes unstable because of increase in neutron to protons ratio, and which makes the nuclide unstable.
- So the nuclei decay by releasing ß-particle ($_{-1}e^0$), this reduces neutron to protons ratio and increases the atomic number by 1.
- Therefore the new element forms with higher atomic number.
- Examples of synthesis of transuranic elements are shown in image.

Transuranium Elements

Elements beyond 92 *(transuranium)* made starting with an γ reaction

$$^{238}_{92}U + ^{1}_{0}n \longrightarrow ^{239}_{92}U + \gamma$$

$$^{239}_{92}U \longrightarrow ^{239}_{93}Np + ^{0}_{-1}\beta$$

$$^{239}_{93}Np \longrightarrow ^{239}_{94}Pu + ^{0}_{-1}\beta$$

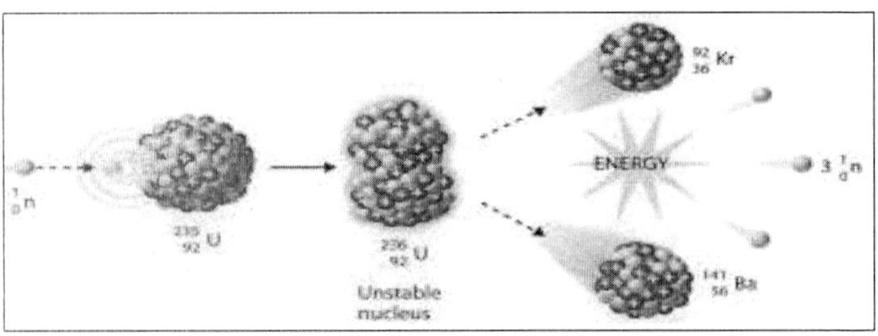

Neutron Bombardment on Uranium

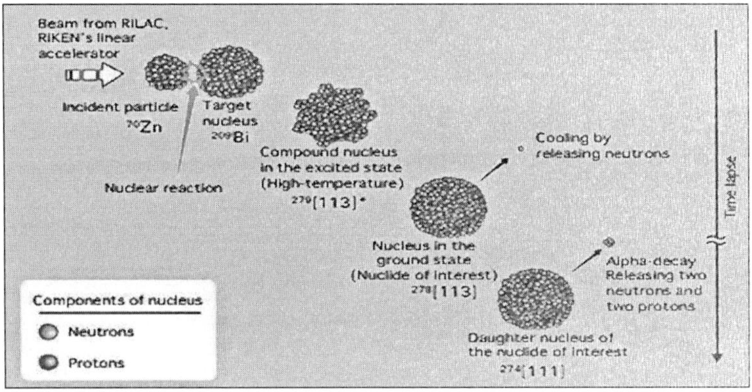

Alpha Decay during Neutron Bombardment

2. Accelerated Projectile Bombardment

- The synthesis of transuranic elements synthsise are carried out by using accelerated projectiles (ionisation energy bombarding particles) Such as $_2He^4$, $_1P^1$ or $_1H^1$, $_1D^2$ etc.
- The addition of $_2He^4$ nucleus on target disturbs the n/p ratio and emits one or more neutrons.
- Eg. $_{94}Pu^{239} + _2He^4 = _{96}Cm^{241} + 2(_0n^1)$

3. Heavy Ion Bombardment

In this process heavy ion required for bombardment and are obtained by removal of extra nuclear electrons from the atoms like $_4Be^9$, $_6C^{12}$, $_7N^{14}$ etc. the resulting positive ion are then accelerated in a cyclotron and used for bombardment on the target elements.

Eg. $_{92}U^{235} + _6C^{12} = _{98}Cf^{246} + 4(_0n^1)$

$_{98}Cf^{250} + _4Be^9 = _{100}Fm^{252} + _2He^4$

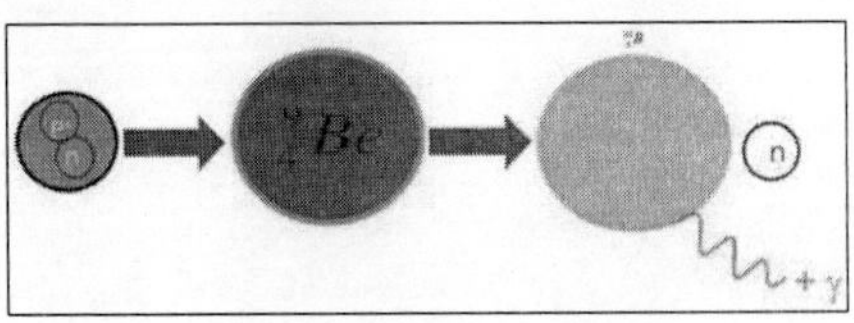

Heavy Ion Bombardment

Chapter - 5

Molecular Orbital Theory (MOT)

Assumption of MOT-

1. Molecular orbitals are formed by the linear combination of atomic orbitals (LCAO's).
2. The number of MO formed is equal to the number of atomic orbitals (AO) combined.
3. The atomic orbitals of two or more atoms combines to form MO's only when they have-

- Close distance
- same energy
- Matching symmetry and geometry.

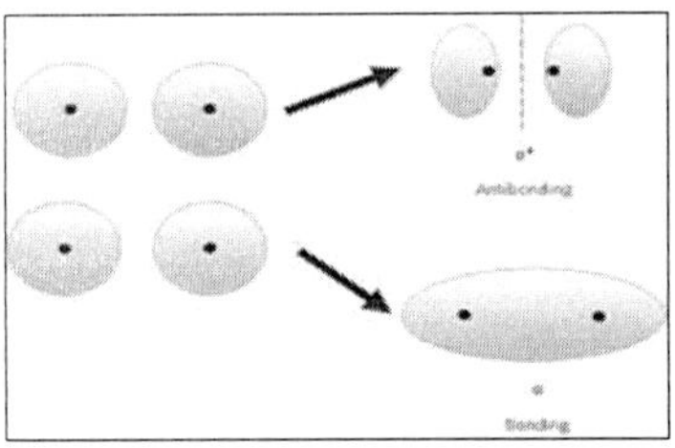

4. The shape of MO depends upon the shape of atomic orbital from which they are formed.

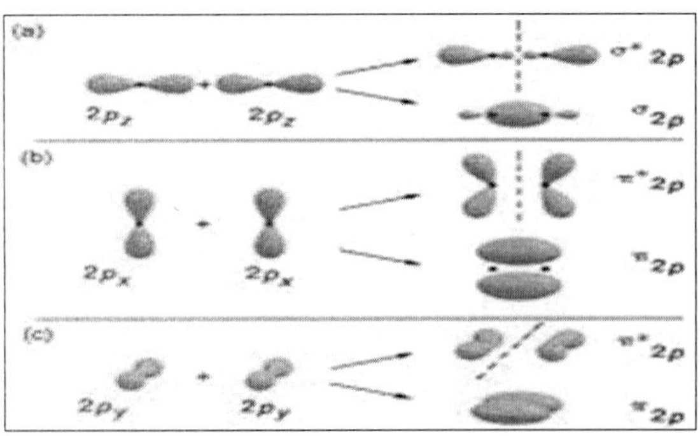

5. Similar to atomic orbital AO.MO's are also denoted by some symbols like σ, σ*, ∏, ∏*......and can be arranged in their increasing order of energies. In homonuclear diatomic molecule the MO in the order of increasing energy are as,

1sσ, 1sσ*, 2sσ, 2sσ*, σ2px, ∏2py, = ∏2pz, ∏*2py, = ∏*2pz, σ*2px....

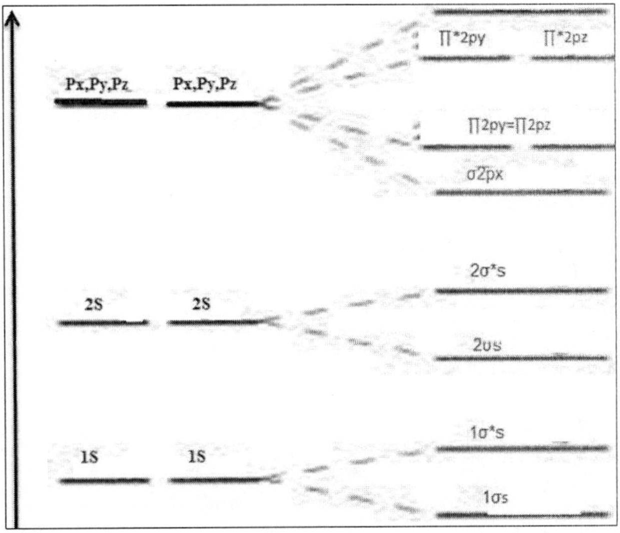

6. Just as we use Aufbau and Pauli's exclusion principle for atoms, we can also use it for the molecule.
7. Each MO is described by a wave function ψ, Known as MO wave function and is obtained by LCAO's.
8. Similar to that of AO's, MO'S possess different energies and shapes.
9. Electrons which are present in MO's are delocalized.
10. Molecular orbitals are polycentric.

Linear Combination of Atomic Orbitals (LCAO's) Method.

1. Orbital is characterized by its wave function (ψ).
2. According to LCAO, the wave function of MO is obtained by either addition or subtraction of ψ of AO.

Atom A and B have Wave function ΨA and ΨB, they can combine in two ways either by ADDITION or by SUBSTRACTION-

$$\Psi_{AB} = N [C_1 \psi_A \pm C_2 \Psi_B]$$

N = Normalising constant.

ψA = Wave function of atom A

ΨB = Wave function of atom B

- There are two ways of combination=
    - In one combination sign of two wave function are similar. It involves addition of Ψ A and ΨB. It forms BMO ψg (gerade)

$$\Psi\ AB = N\ [C1\ \psi A + C2\ \Psi B]$$

    - In other combination two wave function are dissimilar. It involves substraction of Ψ A and ΨB. It forms ABMO ψu(ungerade)

$$\Psi\ AB = N\ [C1\ \psi A - C2\ \Psi B]$$

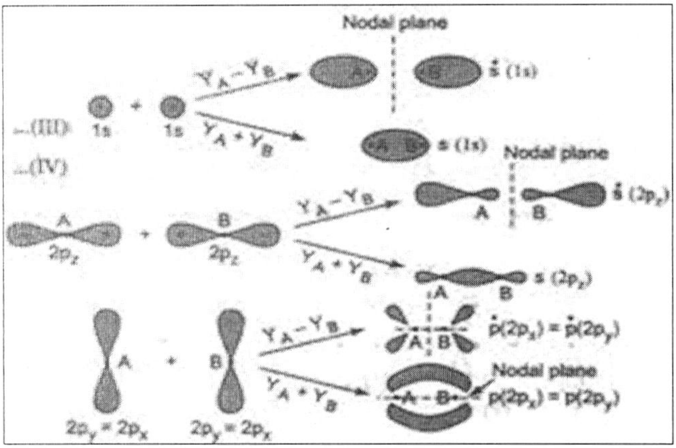

The combination of AO along the axis joining the nuclei produces sigma MO while lateral combination gives Pi ∏ MO.

Considering the combination of s-orbital of atom A with s-orbital of atom B

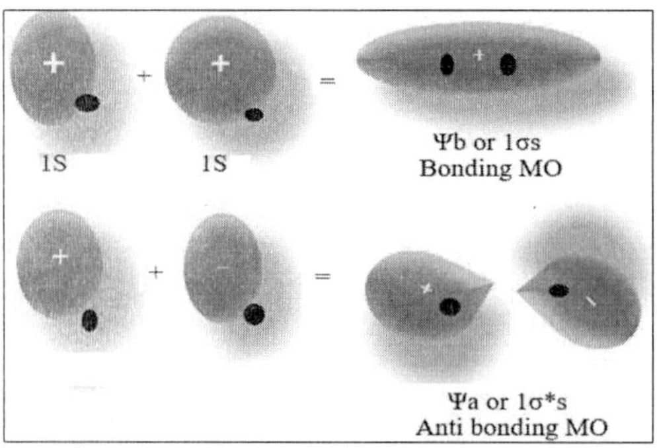

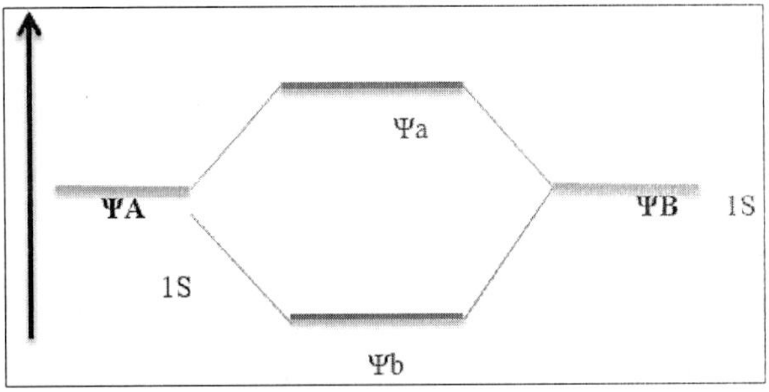

Types of combination or Overlap of AO-

Five types of combination-

1) The S-S Combination of AO
2) The P-P Combination of AO
3) The p-p combination of AO
4) The p-d combination of AO
5) The d-d combination of AO

The s-s Combination of AOs

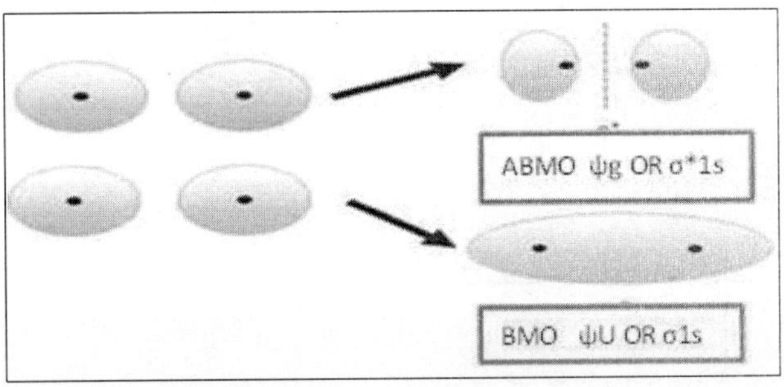

The combination of s-orbitals of one atoms with s-orbitals of other is called S-S overlap or combination and forms BMO and ABMO.

The S-P Combination of AOs

The combination of S-Orbitals of one atom with p- orbitals of other is called s-p combination.

It takes place only when the lobes of p-orbitals are pointing along the axis joining the nuclei.

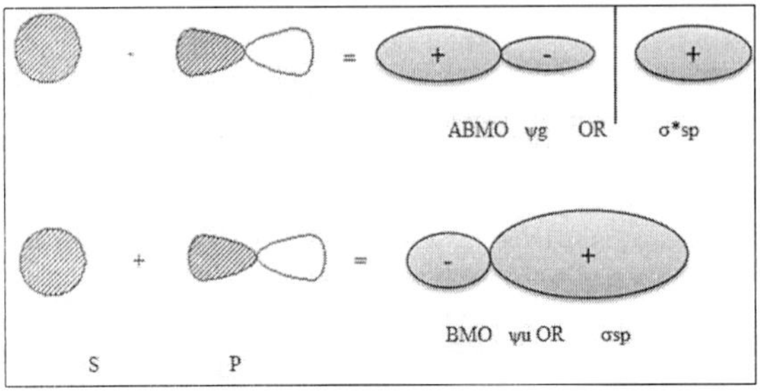

The P-P Combination of Atomic Orbitals

The combination of p-orbital of one atom with p-orbital of other atom.

This overlap may be along axis or lateral.

Formation of Sigma MO: Overlap along the axis forms sigma bonding MO and sigma ABMO

Formation of PI-MO: Sidewise overlap forms Pi MO and Pi ABMO.

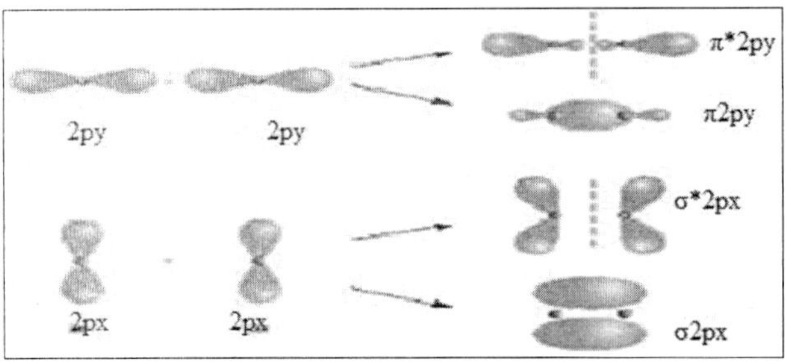

Non-Bonding Combination of Orbitals

In some of the AO combination the energy of atomic orbital and non BMO remain the same is called the non-bonding orbitals.

Eg- s-Py and Py-Pz combination

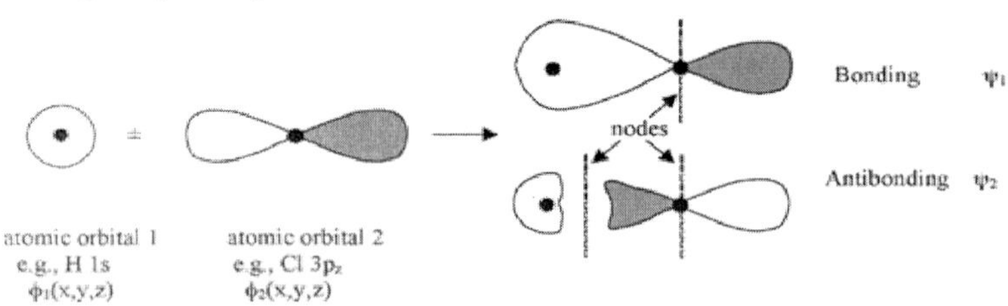

Rules for Filling Electrons to MO's-

1. The MO with lowest energy is filled first. (Aufbau principle).

2. The MO can have maximum of 2 electrons with opposite spin.

3. Pairing of electron will occur only when each orbital of same energy has one electron. (Hund's rule)

4. No two electrons in the same molecule can have same values of all four quantum number. (Pauli exclusion theory).

MO Treatments for Homonuclear Diatomic Molecule-

a) Hydrogen Molecule

Two H atoms combine to form H-molecule

The electronic configuration of H is

- $H_1 = 1S^1$

And

- $H + H = H_2$
- Ionisation energy. 1S + 1S = 1 σ3, 1σ*3

1S- AO of one H is overlaps with 1S-AO of another H atom to form BMO and ABMO.

- The MO-Diagram for H_2 molecule-

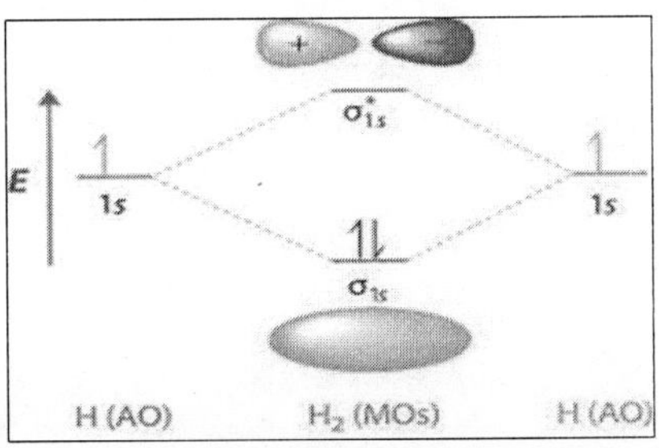

- The electronic configuration for He_2 molecule is- $1\ \sigma s^2, 1\sigma^* s^0$
- The bond order can be calculated as-

Bond order = ½ (Nb-Na)

=1/2 (2-0) = 1

Therefore, H atom are bonded by single bond (H-H)

- The stabilisation energy is calculated by-

S.E = Nb x (-Δ) +Na x (+ Δ)

= - 2Δ + 0Δ = -2Δ

Thus H_2 mlecule is stabilised by 2Δ amount of energy.

- The H- molecule has one paired electrons therefore it is diamagnetic

b) Helium Molecule

- The electronic configuration of He atom is-

  He (2) = $1S^2$

And

- He + He= He_2

  Ionisation energy. 1S + 1S = 1 σs, 1σ*s

- 1S- AO of one He atom is combined with 1S -AO of another He Atom to form BMO and ABMO.

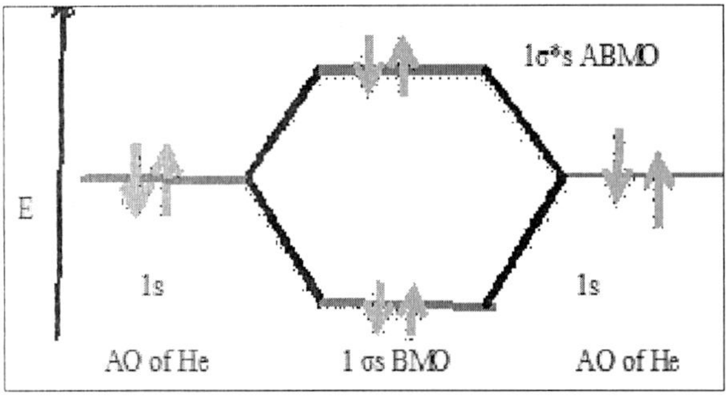

- The electronic configuration of He- Molecule

  He_2 = 1 σs^2, $1\sigma^* s^2$

- The bond order is –

- The bond order can be calculated as-

  Bond order = ½ (Nb-Na)

  =1/2 (2-2) = 0

  Bond order is zero, Therefore, He $_2$ molecule does not exist

- The stabilisation energy is calculated by-

  $$S.E = Nb \times (-\Delta) + Na \times (+\Delta)$$

  $$= -2\Delta + 2\Delta = 0$$

  Thus He2 molecule has zero stabilisation energy.

3. Helium Molecular Ion- (He_2^+)

- The He atom is combined by He^+ ion-

$He + He^+ = He_2^+$

The $He^+{}_2$ ion has only three electrons. Two are in BMO and one are in ABMO.

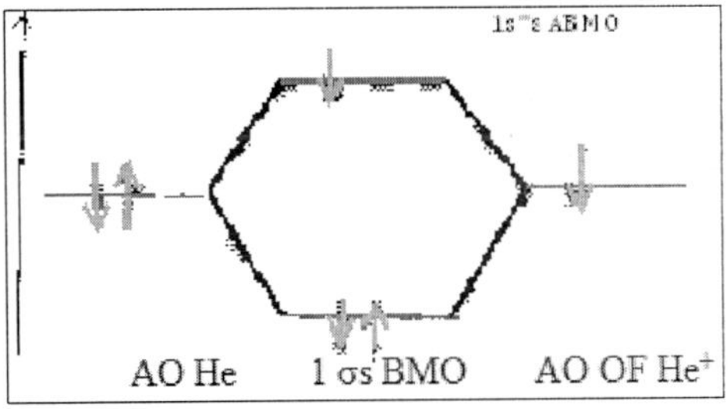

- The bond order is –

The bond order can be calculated as-

Bond order = ½ (Nb-Na)

=1/2 (2-1) = 1/2

Thus, Bond order is half, Therefore, He_2^+ molecule ion exist.

- The stabilisation energy is calculated by-

S.E = Nb x (-Δ) +Na x (+ Δ)

= - 2Δ + 1Δ = -Δ

Thus He_2^+ molecule has -Δ stabilisation energy.

4. Lithium Molecule (Li_2)

This molecule is formed by combination of two Li atom

$Li + Li = Li_2$

The electronic configuration of Li atom is-

Li (3) = $1S^2$, $2S^2$

Here the outer AO will overlap and form MO while inner AO will not combined.

$Li + Li = Li_2$

$2S^2 + 2S^2 = 2\sigma s, 2\sigma^* s$

The MO diagram of Li- molecule-

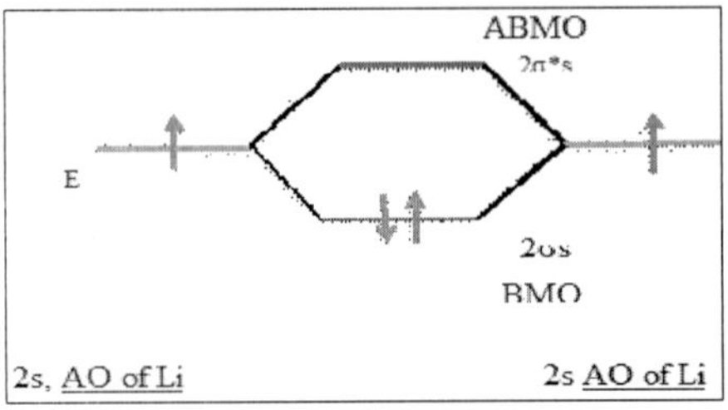

Electronic Configuration of Li-Molecule

$Li_2 = 2\sigma s^2, 2\sigma^* s^0$

- **The Bond Order for Li Molecule**

  Bond order = ½ (Nb-Na)

  =1/2 (2-0) = 1

  Thus, Bond order is ONE, Therefore, Li molecule is formed by single bond

- **The Stabilisation Energy is Calculated by**

  S.E = Nb x (-Δ) +Na x (+ Δ)

  = - 2Δ + 0xΔ = -2Δ

  Thus Li molecule has -2Δ stabilisation energy.

- **Magnetism-** Li has paired electron therefore it is diamagnetic.

Explaination

The Li molecule is analogous to H_2 molecule. The bond in Li_2 is longer than H_2, because the 2S orbital of Li is larger in size and more diffuse than 1S orbital of H. so there overlap is poor and this make larger bond length.

5. **Beryllium Molecule- (Be_2)**

The Electronic configuration of be atom is,

$Be (4) = 1S^2, 2S^2, 2P^0$

The be molecule is formed by,

$Be + Be = Be_2$

Here the outer AO will overlap and form MO while inner AO will not combined.

Ionisation energy., $2s + 2s = 2\sigma s, 2\sigma^* s$

Each 2S of be atom provides 2 electron therefore there are total 4 electron in be molecule.

The MO diagram for be molecule

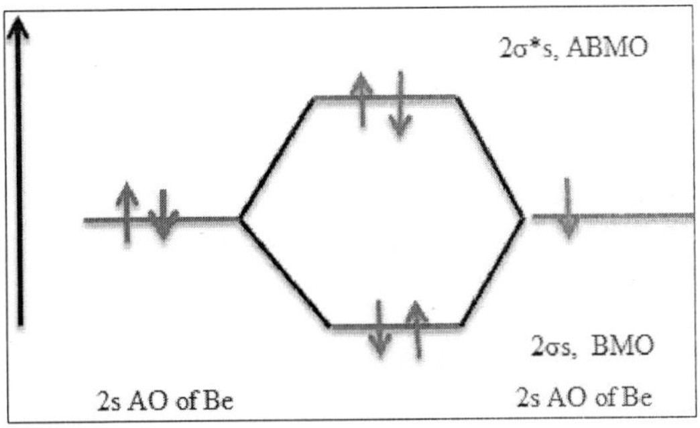

- Electronic configuration of Li- molecule

  $Be_2 = 2\sigma s^2, 2\sigma^* s^2$

- The bond order for Li molecule-

  Bond order = ½ (Nb-Na)

  =1/2 (2-2) = 0

- Thus, Bond order is zero, Therefore, Be molecule does not formed.

- The stabilisation energy is calculated by-

  S.E = Nb x (-Δ) +Na x (+ Δ)

  = - 2xΔ + 2xΔ = 0

Thus Be_2 molecule has zero stabilization energy. Therefore be molecule is non-existing molecule.

6. Boron Molecule- (B_2)

- The Electronic configuration of Be atom is,

  B (5) = $1s^2, 2s^2, 2Px^1, 2py^0, 2pz^0$

- The B molecule is formed by,

  $B + B = B_2$

Here the outer 2s and 2p AO will overlap and form MO while inner AO will not combined.

Ionisation energy, 2s + 2s = 2σs, 2σ*s

2px + 2px = σ2px, σ*2px

2py +2py = π2py, π*2py

$2pz + 2pz = \pi 2pz, \pi^* 2pz$

A.O = MOLECULAR ORBITAL

Each 2S of B atom provides 2 electrons while each 2px AO provides one electron, therefore there are total 6 electron in B_2 molecule.

The MO Diagram for B Molecule

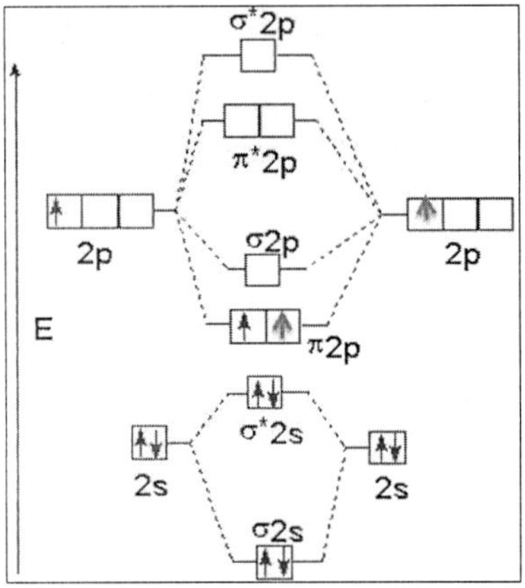

- Electronic configuration of Li- molecule

  $B_2 = KK, 2\sigma s^2, 2\sigma^* s^2, \pi 2py^1 = \pi 2pz^1$

- The bond order for Boron molecule-

  Bond order = ½ (Nb-Na)

  = 1/2 (4-2)

  = 2/2 = 1

- Thus, Bond order is one, therefore, two B atom are bonded by single bond.

- The stabilisation energy is calculated by-

  $S.E = Nb \times (-\Delta) + Na \times (+\Delta)$

  $= -4 \times \Delta + 2 \times \Delta = -2\Delta$

Thus B_2 molecule has 2 Δ stabilisation energy.

- Magnetism - Boron molecule has two unpaired electrons therefore it is paramagnetic.

7. **Nitrogen Molecule- (N_2)**

The nitrogen molecule is formed by combination of two Nitrogen atoms.

The electronic configuration of N atom is-

N (7) = $1s^2$, $2s^2$, $2Px^1$, $2py^1$, $2pz^1$

- The N molecule is formed by,

N + N = N2

Here the outer 2s and 2p AO will overlap and form MO while inner AO will not combined.

ionisation energy., 2s + 2s = $2\sigma s$, $2\sigma^*s$

2px + 2px = $\sigma 2px$, σ^*2px

2py +2py = $\pi 2py$, π^*2py

2pz +2pz = $\pi 2pz$, π^*2pz

A.O M.O

Each 2S of N atom provides 2 electrons while each 2px, 2py and 2pz AO provides three electrons, therefore there are total 10 electron in N2 molecule.

- Electronic configuration of N_2 - molecule

  B2 = KK, $2\sigma s^2$, $2\sigma^*s^2$, $\pi 2py^2 = \pi 2pz^2$, $\sigma 2px^2$

- The bond order for N_2 molecule-

  Bond order = ½ (Nb-Na)

  = 1/2 (8-2)

  = 6/2

  = 3

- Thus, Bond order is three, therefore, two N atom are bonded by Triple bond. N≡N

- The stabilisation energy is calculated by-

  S.E = Nb x (-Δ) +Na x (+ Δ)

  = - 8xΔ + 2xΔ = -6Δ

Thus B2 molecule has 6Δ stabilisation energy.

- **Magnetism-** Nitrogen molecule has all paired electrons therefore it is diamagnetic.

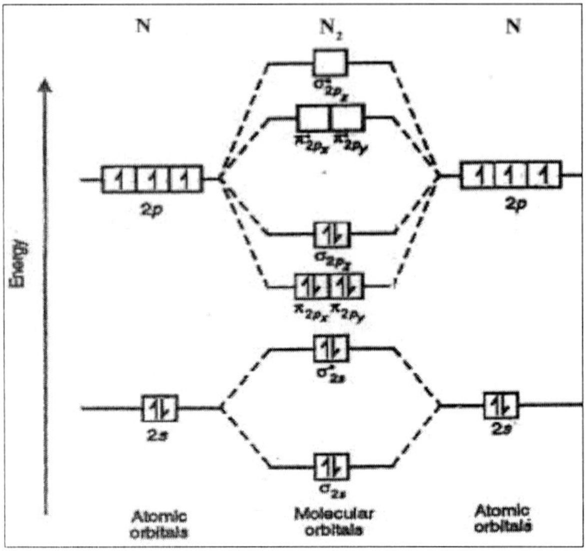

Fig: Molecular orbital energy level diagram of N_2

- **Fluorine Molecule- (F_2)**

The fluorine molecule is formed by combination of two fluorine atoms.

The electronic configuration of F atom is-

F (9) = $1s^2$. $2s^2$, $2Px^2$, $2py^2$, $2pz^1$

The F molecule is formed by,

$F + F = F_2$

Here the outer 2s and 2p AO will overlap and form MO while inner AO will not combined.

Ionisation energy, 2s + 2s = 2σs, 2σ*s

2px + 2px = σ2px, σ*2px

2py +2py = π2py, π*2py

2pz +2pz = π2pz, π*2pz

A.O = MOLECULAR ORBITAL

Each 2S of F atom provides 2 electrons while each 2px, 2py and 2pz AO provides FIVE electrons, therefore there are total 14 electron in F_2 molecule.

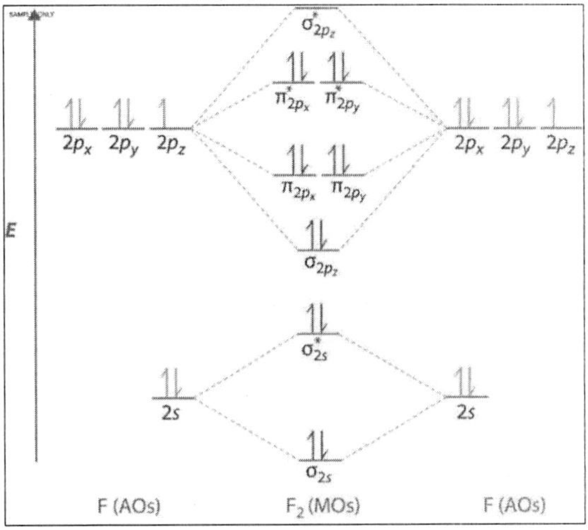

- Electronic configuration of F_2 – molecule

  F_2 = KK, $2\sigma s^2$, $2\sigma^* s^2$, $\sigma 2px^2$, $\pi 2py^2 = \pi 2pz^2$, $\pi 2py^2 = \pi 2pz^2$

- The bond order for F2 molecule-

  Bond order = ½ (Nb-Na)

  = 1/2 (8-6)

  = 2/2

  =1

- Thus, Bond order is ONE, Therefore, two F atom are bonded by Triple bond. F-F

- The stabilisation energy is calculated by-

  S.E = Nb x (-Δ) +Na x (+ Δ)

  = - 8xΔ + 6xΔ = -2Δ

  Thus F2 molecule has 2Δ stabilisation energy.

- **Magnetism**- Fluorine molecule has all paired electrons therefor it is diamagnetic.

MO Treatment for Hetero Nuclear Diatomic Molecule

The molecules formed by the two different atoms are called as hetero diatomic Molecule.

Eg. CO, NO, HCl etc.

Formation of Heterodiatomic Molecule

1. Carbon Monoxide (CO)

The carbon mono oxide is formed by combination of one carbon and one Oxygen atom.

The electronic configuration of C and O atoms are-

C (6) = $1s^2, 2s^2, 2Px^1, 2py^1, 2pz^0$

O (8) = $1s^2, 2s^2, 2Px^2, 2py^1, 2pz^1$

Thus there is 4 and 6 electron in the valence shell of C and O atoms respectively. Therefore total number of 10 electrons is there in the CO molecule.

The CO molecule is formed by,

C + O = CO

Here the outer 2s and 2p AO will overlap and form MO while inner AO will not combined.

Ionisation energy, 2s + 2s = $2\sigma s, 2\sigma^* s$

2px + 2px = $\sigma 2px, \sigma^* 2px$

2py +2py = $\pi 2py, \pi^* 2py$

2pz +2pz = $\pi 2pz, \pi^* 2pz$

A.O = M.O

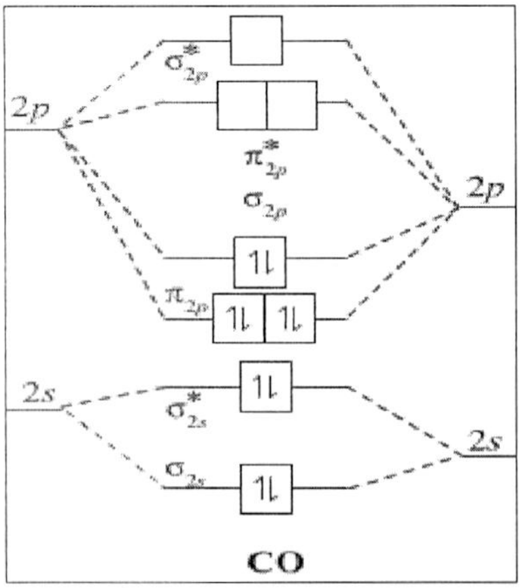

The O is more electronegative than carbon, hence in MO diagram AO of O atom is at lower energy level than AO of C.

- Electronic configuration of CO – molecule

  $CO = KK, 2\sigma s^2, 2\sigma^* s^2, \pi 2py^2 = \pi 2pz^2, \sigma 2px^2$

- The bond order for CO molecule-

  Bond order = ½ (Nb-Na)

  = 1/2 (8-2)

  = 6/2

  =3

- Thus, Bond order is THREE, Therefore, C and O atom are bonded by Triple bond. C≡O
- The stabilisation energy is calculated by-

  S.E = Nb x (-Δ) +Na x (+ Δ)

  = - 8xΔ + 2xΔ = -6Δ

  Thus CO molecule has 6Δ stabilisation energy.

- Magnetism- CO molecule has all paired electrons therefor it is diamagnetic.

CO molecule is polar-

This is because the presence of more electrons in BMO is closer to Oxygen than carbon. This makes more shift of negative charge toward oxygen and carbon becomes positively charge. Therefore it is polar.

CO is isoelectronic with N_2–

Isoelectronic species have similar MO and molecular structure. And CO and N_2 molecule has same MO and molecular structure therefore they are isoelectronic.

- **Nitric Oxide (NO) Molecule**

  It is formed by the combination of one N and one O atom.

  The electronic configuration of N and O is-

  N (7) - $1s^2, 2s^2, 2Px^1, 2py^1, 2pz^1$

  O (8) = $1s^2, 2s^2, 2Px^2, 2py^1, 2pz^1$

  Thus there is 5 and 6 electron in the valence shell of N and O atoms respectively. Therefore total number of 11 electrons is there in the NO molecule.

The NO molecule is formed by,

$$N + O = NO$$

Here the outer 2s and 2p AO will overlap and form MO while inner AO will not combined.

Ionisation energy, 2s + 2s = 2σs, 2σ*s

2px + 2px = σ2px, σ*2px

2py +2py = π2py, π*2py

2pz +2pz = π2pz, π*2pz

A.O M.O

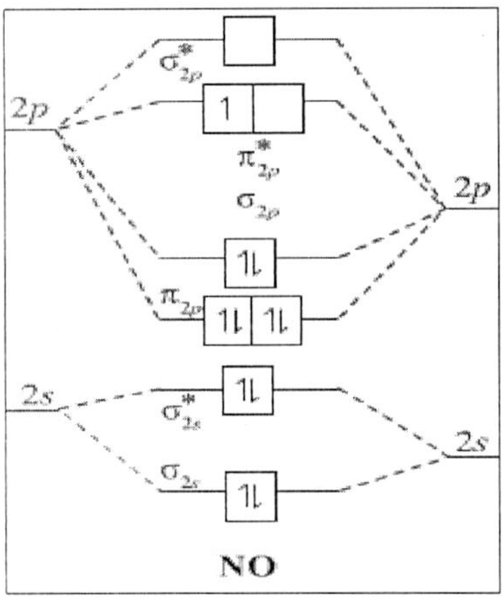

The O is more electronegative than carbon, hence in MO diagram AO of O atom is at lower energy level than AO of N.

- Electronic configuration of CO – molecule

  NO = KK, $2\sigma s^2$, $2\sigma^* s^2$, $\pi 2py^2 = \pi 2pz^2$, $\sigma 2px^2$, $\pi^* 2py^1 = \pi^* 2pz^0$

- The bond order for NO molecule-

  Bond order = ½ (Nb-Na)

  = 1/2 (8-3)

  = 5/2

  =2.5

- Thus, Bond order is 2.5, Therefore, N and O atom are bonded by one sigma, one pi and one three electron bond.

- The stabilisation energy is calculated by-

  S.E = Nb x (-Δ) +Na x (+ Δ)

  = - 8xΔ + 3xΔ = -5Δ

Thus NO molecule has 5Δ stabilisation energy.

- Magnetism- NO molecule has one unpaired electrons therefore it is paramagnetic.

3. **Nitrosyl Ion- (NO+ Ion)**

It is formed by removal of one electron from π*2py ABMO of NO molecule.

$NO = NO + e^-$

The electronic configuration of NO+ ion is –

$NO+ = KK, 2\sigma s^2, 2\sigma^* s^2, \pi 2py^2 = \pi 2pz^2, \sigma 2px^2,$

- Bond order-
- The bond order for NO+ ion-

  Bond order = ½ (Nb-Na)

  = 1/2 (8-2)

  = 6/2

  =3

- Thus, Bond order is 3, Therefore, N and O atom are bonded by triple bond.
- The stabilisation energy is calculated by-

  S.E = Nb x (-Δ) +Na x (+ Δ)

  = - 8xΔ + 2xΔ = -6Δ

  Thus NO + ion has 6Δ stabilisation energy.

- **Magnetism-** NO+ ion has all paired electrons therefore it is diamagnetic.

Due to higher bond order the NO+ ion has shorter and stronger bond than neutral NO molecule. Therefore it is more stable than NO molecule.

4. **Hydrogen Chloride (HCI)-**

It is formed by combination of one H and on Cl atom.

$H = 1S^2$

$Cl = 1s2, 2s^2, 2P^6, 3s^2, 3px^1, 3py^1, 3pz^1$

- In HCl, the inner AO of Cl do not take part in bonding and remain in nonbonding state. Thus the outer 3p involved in bonding with 1s AO of H, which has comparable energies.
- Only 3px of Cl is of corresponding symmetry pointing along the molecular axis, so only 3px of Cl is suitable for bonding.
- Therefore the combination of 1s AO of H atom with 3px AO of Cl take place and form σ MO and denoted as σsp BMO and σ*sp ABMO.

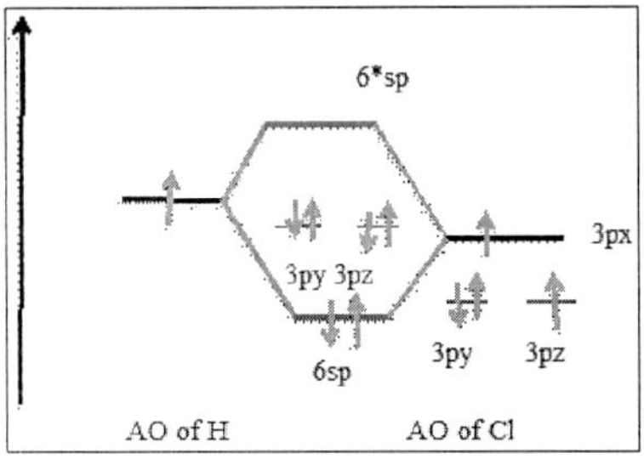

The electronic confiburation of NO+ ion is –

HCl = KL, [σsp^2]

- Bond order-

  The bond order for HCl -

  Bond order = ½ (Nb-Na)

  = 1/2 (2-0)

  = 2/2

  =1

- Thus, Bond order is 1, Therefore, H and Cl atom are bonded by single bond.
- The stabilisation energy is calculated by-

  S.E = Nb x (-Δ) +Na x (+ Δ)

  = - 2xΔ + 0xΔ = -2Δ

  Thus NO+ ion has 2Δ stabilisation energy.

- Magnetism- HCl has all paired electrons therefore it is diamagnetic.

HCl is a polar molecule, because Cl is more electronegative than H. AO of Cl is nearer to the σsp BMO, hence electrons are more closer toward Cl atom, which makes Cl slightly negative and H slightly positive. This causes HCl is polar molecule.

MCQ Practice

1. **The Filling of Molecular Orbital Takes Place According to**

   a) The Aufbau Principle

   b) Pauli Exculsion Principle

   c) Hund's rule of maximum multiplicity

   d) All of the mentioned

2. **Bond Order of O_2, F_2, N_2 respectively are**

   a) +1, +2, +3

   b) +2, +3, +1

   c) **+2, +1, +3**

   d) +3, +2, +1

3. **On the Basis of Molecular Orbital Theory, Select the Most Appropriate Option**

   a) The bond order of O_2 is 2.5 and it is paramagnetic.

   b) The bond order of O_2 is 1.5 and it is paramagnetic.

   c) **The bond order of O_2 is 2 and it is diamagnetic.**

   d) The bond order of O_2 is 2 and it is paramagnetic.

4. **Which of the Following Molecule does not Exist Due to its Zero Bond Order?**

   a) H_2^+

   b) He_2^+

   c) **He_2**

   d) H_2^-

5. **According to Molecular Orbital Theory, the shape and size of a Molecular Orbital Depends Upon**

   a) Shape and size of the combining atomic orbitals.

   b) Numbers of the combining atomic orbitals.

   c) Orientation of the combining atomic orbitals.

   d) All of the mentioned.

6. **Choose the Incorrect Statement from the Following Options.**

   a) **In bonding molecular orbital, electron density is low in the region** between the nuclei of bonded atoms.

b) The energy of antibonding molecular orbital is higher than that of atomic orbitals from which it is formed.

c) Every electron in bonding molecular orbital contributes toward stability of the molecule.

d) Antibonding takes place when lobes of atomic orbitals have different signs.

7. **What is the Molecular Geometry for Ammonia (NH3)?**

a) saw horse

b) trigonal planar

c) tetrahedral

d) pyramidal

8. **Antibonding Molecular Orbitals are produced by**

a) Constructive interaction of atomic orbitals.

b) Destructive interaction of atomic orbitals.

c) the overlap of the atomic orbitals of two negative ions

d) all of these

9. **Which Statement is false? A Sigma Molecular Orbital**

a) May result from overlap of p atomic orbitals perpendicular to the molecular axis (side-on).

b) May result from overlap of p atomic orbitals along the molecular axis (head-on).

c) May result from overlap of two s atomic orbitals.

d) May result from overlap of one s and one p atomic orbitals.

e) May be either bonding or antibonding.

10. **Carbon Monoxide Has Ten Bonding Electrons and four Antibonding Electrons. Therefore it Has a Bond Order of**

a) 3

b) 7

c) 1

d) 5/2

e) 2

Chapter - 6

The Chemistry of Transition Elements

Introduction

Definition- The elements in which last electrons enters into d-orbital of penultimate shell [(n-1) d shell] are called as d-block elements.

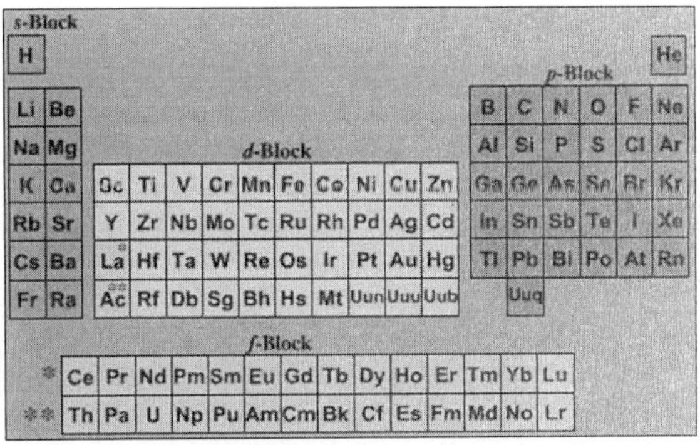

Classification of D-Block Elements

These elements are classified in 4 series-

- First or 3d series- 10 elements [Sc (21) to Zn(30)]
- Second or 4d series- 10 elements [Y (39) TO Cd (48)]
- Third or 5d series- 10 elements [La(57) to Hf (72)]
- Fourth or 6d series- 10 elements [Ac(89) to Rf (104)}

Position of D-Block Element in Periodic Table

1. Present between s-block and p-block elements.
2. In 4th. 5th, 6th, and 7th periods of periodic table.
3. From group III B (3) TO II B (12) Group.

Transition Elements

1. These are d-block elements.
2. The penultimate d- sub shell is incomplete.

3. Have Variables oxidation states.

4. They are called transition elements because they are present in between s-block and p-block.

5. The general electronic configuration is $(n-1)d^{1-10}, n\ S^{0,1,2}$

6. Zinc, cadmium, mercury and copernicium are not d-block element because of completely filled d-orbital (d-10).

Electronic Configuration of Transition Element

3d-Series			4d-Series			5d-Series		
At. no.	Element	Electronic configuration	At. no.	Element	Electronic configuration	At. no.	Element	Electronic configuration
21	Sc	$[Ar]3d^1 4s^2$	39	Y	$[Kr]4d^1 5s^2$	57	La	$[Xe]5d^1 6s^2$
22	Ti	$[Ar]3d^2 4s^2$	40	Zr	$[Kr]4d^2 5s^2$	72	Hf	$[Xe]4f^{14} 5d^2 6s^2$
23	V	$[Ar]3d^3 4s^2$	41	Nb	$[Kr]4d^4 5s^1$	73	Ta	$[Xe]4f^{14} 5d^3 6s^2$
24	Cr	$[Ar]3d^5 4s^1$	42	Mo	$[Kr]4d^5 5s^1$	74	W	$[Xe]4f^{14} 5d^4 6s^2$
25	Mn	$[Ar]3d^5 4s^2$	43	Tc	$[Kr]4d^5 5s^2$	75	Re	$[Xe]4f^{14} 5d^5 6s^2$
26	Fe	$[Ar]3d^6 4s^2$	44	Ru	$[Kr]4d^7 5s^1$	76	Os	$[Xe]4f^{14} 5d^6 5s^2$
27	Co	$[Ar]3d^7 4s^2$	45	Rh	$[Kr]4d^8 5s^1$	77	Ir	$[Xe]4f^{14} 5d^7 6s^2$
28	Ni	$[Ar]3d^8 4s^2$	46	Pd	$[Kr]4d^{10} 5s^0$	78	Pt	$[Xe]4f^{14} 5d^9 6s^1$
29	Cu	$[Ar]3d^{10} 4s^1$	47	Ag	$[Kr]4d^{10} 5s^1$	79	Au	$[Xe]4f^{14} 5d^{10} 6s^1$
30	Zn	$[Ar]3d^{10} 4s^2$	48	Cd	$[Kr]4d^{10} 5s^2$	80	Hg	$[Xe]4f^{14} 5d^{10} 6s^2$

Electronic Configuration of First Series of Transition Element

1. Last two shells 3d and 4s are incomplete.

2. Regular filling of 3d subshell, but irregularity in Cr and Cu.

   Ionisation energy. Cr (24) = $[Ar]\ 3d^5, 4s^1$

   Cu (29) = $[Ar]\ 3d^{10}, 4s^1$

3. This is due to more stability of half-filled d-5 shell and completely filled d-10 shell.

4. 3d shell completed at Cu.

5. General electronic configuration of 3d-

   [Ar] 3d 1-10, 4s1-2

6. The electronic configuration of Zn(30) = [Ar] 3d10,4s2

Electronic Configuration of Second Transition Series

1. It contain element from yttrium to cadmium.

2. The general electronic configuration of 4d series [Kr] 4d1-10,n S,0,1,2.
3. The number of electron in 4d shell varies from 1-10 as we move from Yttrium to cadmium.
4. The Cadmium atom and its ion (Cd+2) has a complete 4d shell therefore it is not transition element. Cd (48) = [Kr] 4d10,5S2 Cd (+2) (46) = [Kr] 4d10,5s0

General Characteristics of D-Block Elements

Metallic Properties

1. Metallic and non-metallic character are depends on electronic configuration of element.
2. They are good conductor of heat and electricity.
3. They are malleable and ductile.
4. They form alloys with many other metals.
5. They are hard and brittle except mercury.
6. Cu, Ag and Au are very good conductor of heat and electricity.
7. They have high density and low atomic volume.
8. They form colored and magnetic compounds.
9. They form both covalent and metallic bonds

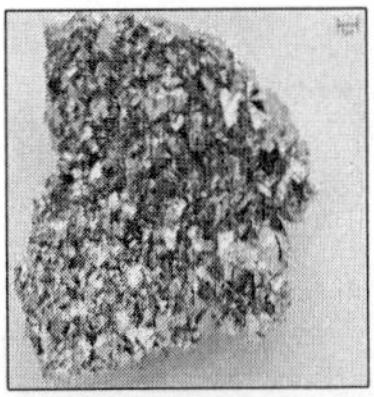

Hard and brittle

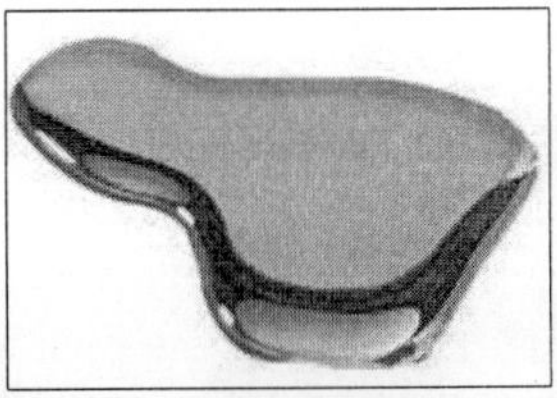

Mercury

Malleable

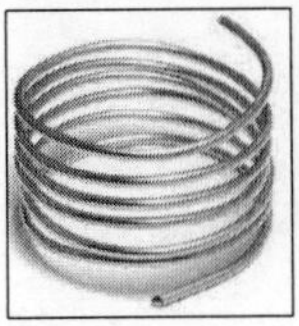

Ductile

Alloy

Coloured d-Elements

Molar Volumes and Densities

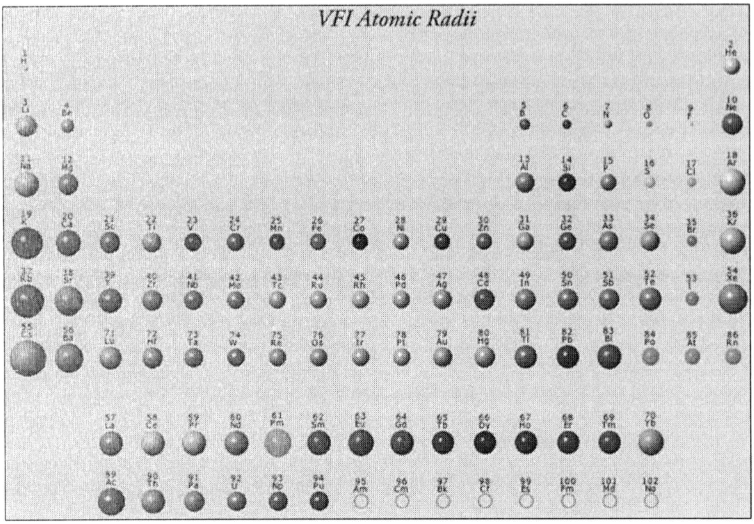

1. They have lower molar volumes and high densities then S and P block elements.
2. As atomic no. increases, extra electrons added in d-orbital and extra protons in nucleus. These extra protons attracts all electrons and decrease the atomic volume.
3. Density increases with decrease in atomic volume.
4. Therefore density of transition element is high, Except Scandium, titanium and yttrium.

3-Atomic Radii

1. D-Block elements have smaller size than s-block element and larger size than p-block element.
2. In period, atomic size of transition element decreases from left to right.
3. This is due to-
   a) Addition of electron in d-orbital.
   b) The electrons from last shell are pulled towards nucleus and cause shrinkage.

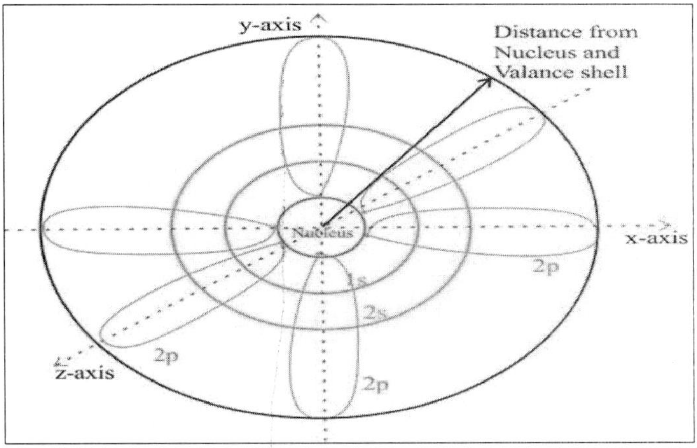

- In a group, size of element increases top to bottom due to increase in number of shell.
- The size of second series and third series are nearly similar, due to lanthanoid contraction.
- E.g- Zr and Hf, Nb and Ta, Mo and W, Tc and Re have similar size, hence similar chemical and physical properties, therefore they are called as chemical twins.

Ionic Radii

- The ionic radii follow the same trend as atomic radii.
- The ionic radii decreases with increase in charge on the ion.

Melting Point and Boiling Point

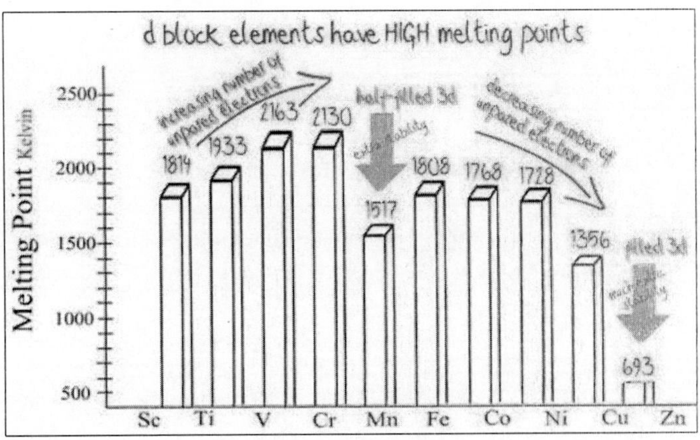

- melting point and boiling point are very high., due to-
    1. Closely packed crystal structure.
    2. Partly filled d-sub shell, which cause strong covalent bonding.
- The transition element melts above 900^0C.
- Tungsten (W) have highest melting point 3410^0C.
- Zn, Cd and Hg have low melting point 420^0C, $321C^0$, And -39^0C.

Due to,

1. Completely filled d- orbitals.
2. Absence of covalent bond.

Ionization Energies

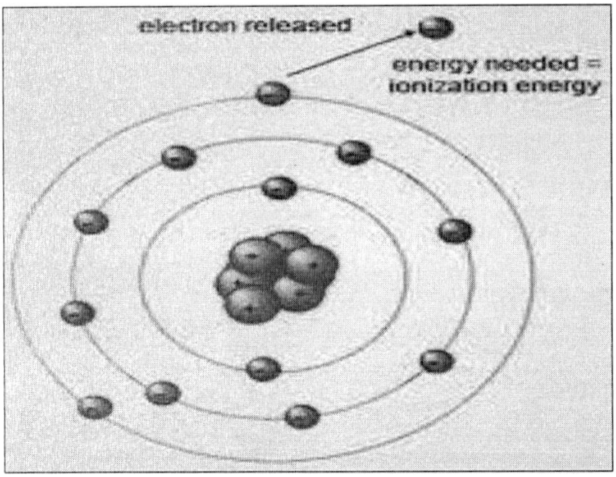

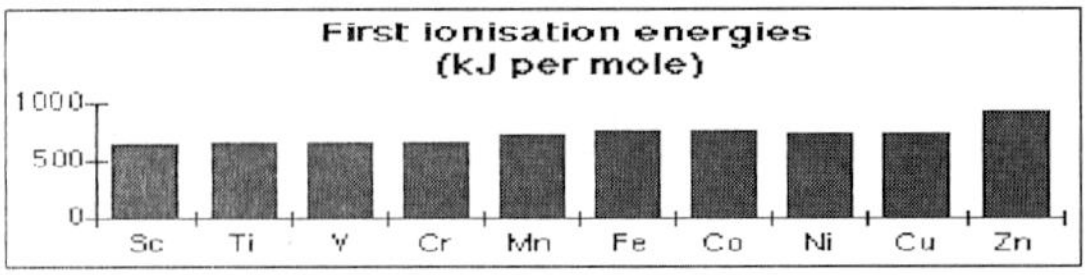

1. The energy required to remove outermost electrons are called ionization energy.
2. Its unit is KJ/Mole.
3. Due to small size, the ionization energy of d-block element is high.
4. For d-block element, ionization energy is in between s-block and p-block.

5. D-block element are less electropositive then s-block and more electropositive then p-block.
6. Along period, the ionisation energy of d-block elements are increases from left to right, due decrease in size from left to right.
7. The Zn has much higher ionisation energy due to completely filled 3d-orbital (stable configuration d-10).
8. The factor affecting ionisation energy is-

1. The size of atom.
2. The charge on nucleus.
3. Shielding effect (screening) of inner electrons from nuclear charge.
4. The type of electrons remove (s,p,d &f).

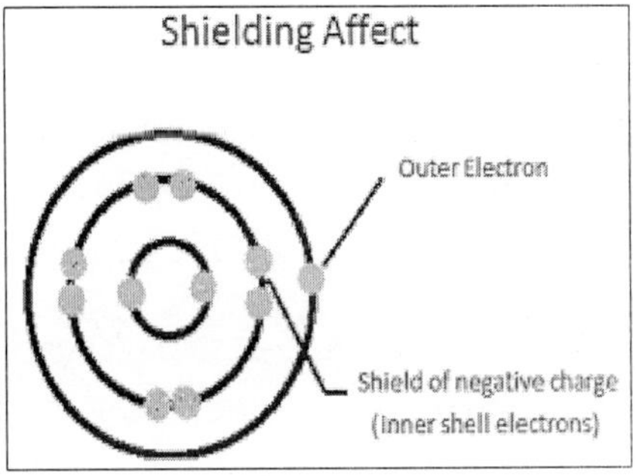

Reactivity-

1. They react with mineral acids (HCl, H2SO4, HNO3) and liberate H2gas.
2. Few of d-block elements are noble (Pt and Au).
3. In general they are less reactive.

Due to-

1. The small atomic size.
2. High ionization energy.
3. High melting point.
4. High heat of sublimation due to covalent bonding.
5. Low heat of hydration.

Oxidation States

Definition-

"The charge left on the central atom when all the other atoms of the compound are removed".

- The O.S of Sin $H_2 SO_4$ is given as-

  The O has (-II) O.S, H has (+1) O.S'

Then sum of Oxidation no. of all the atoms in $H_2 SO_4$ is ZERO

$2 (H) + S + 4(O) = 0$

$2^* (+1) + X + 4^* (-2) = 0$

$+2 + X - 8 = 0$

$X = +6$

Therefore O.S of Sin $H_2 SO_4 = +6$

- Similarly, the oxidation state of Mn in KMnO4 = +7
- The transition element shows large no. of O.S related to their electronic configuration.

Standard Electrode Potential

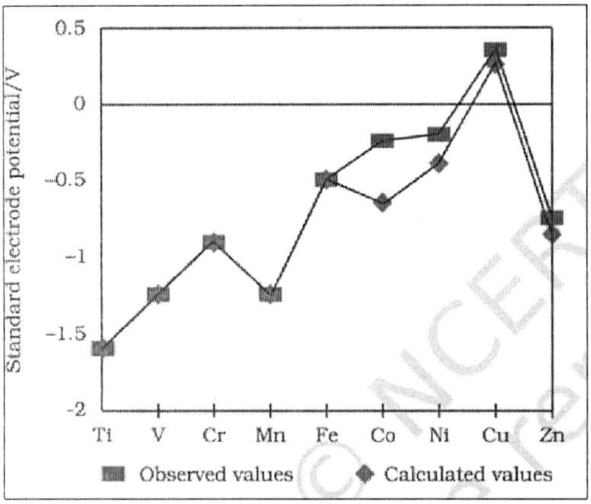

1. Definition-

   The potential developed at the single electrode at 298 K due to half-cell reaction when an electrode is dipped in its salt solution having unit activity.

2. The Standard electrode potential of H is ZERO.
3. The Standard electrode potential of d-block is higher than H.
4. THE Standard oxidation potential of First transition series is much higher than Standard hydrogen electrode except Cu.

Reducing Properties

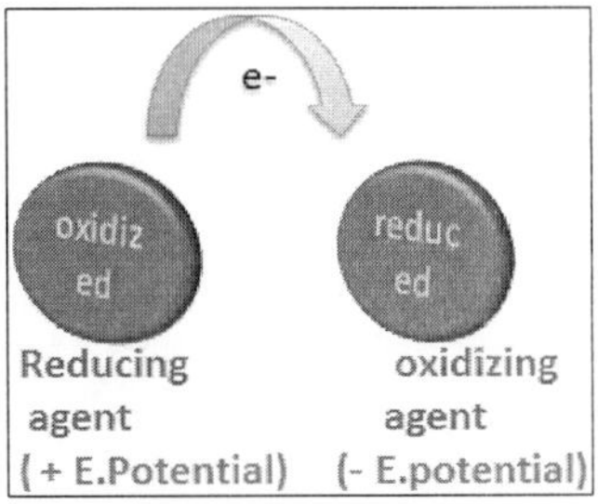

- The reducing agent always loses electrons.
- Except copper all the transition element have higher value of standard oxidation potential than Standard Hydrogen Electrode.
- Hence these element loose electron easily and can reduce other ions.

  $M \rightarrow M^{2+} + 2e-$
- Therefore they are good reducing agent.
- They are less powerful reducing agent than s - block element.

Due to-

- They have high Ionisation Energy.
- Have high heat of vaporization.
- Low heat of hydration.
- Cu has negative oxidation potential, this means it cannot displace H^+ from Acids.

  Hence Cu is poor reducing agents.

Color-

Most of transition element is colored.

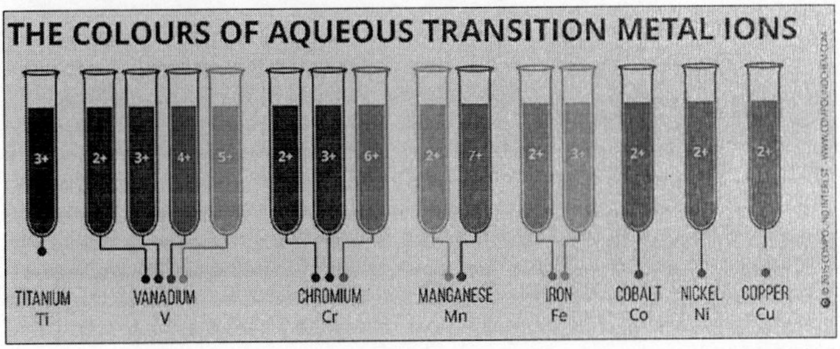

Due to-

1) Charge transfer transition
2) d-d transition of electrons

D-D transition of Electrons-

- The transition of electrons from lower energy d-orbital to higher energy d-orbital with in same shell is called d-d transitions.

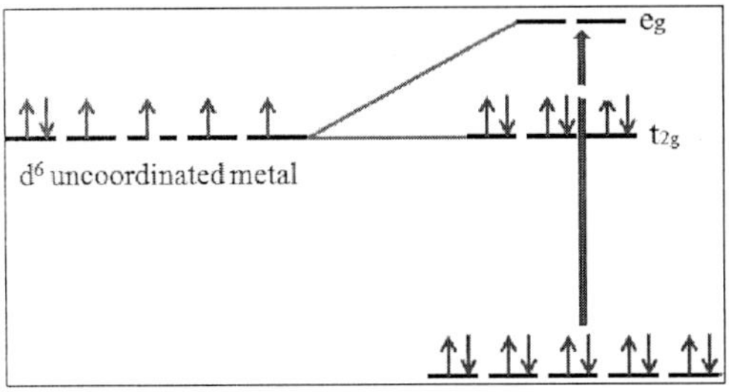

- When complex compound is formed the degeneracy of d-orbital splits into two or more set.
- Some are at higher energy level while some are at lower energy level.
- The d-d electrons excitation takes place from lower level to higher level by absorbing light energy and hence the complex compounds appears colored.
- E.G- $[Ti\,(H_2O)6]^3$ shows purple color.
- The color is shown by partly filled d-orbital (d^{1-9}) due to d-d transition.
- Eg Co^{2+} (d^2) = pink,
- Cr^{2+} (d^3)= bluish green
- Ni^{2+} (d^8)= green color
- The metals having vacant (d0) or completely filled (d10) shell are colourless.

Eg. Sc^{3+}, Ti^{4+} have (d0) and Zn^{2+}, Cu+ have (d10) configuration and are colorless.

Charge Transfer Transitions

Some transition element shows color due to charge transfer transitions. In this, the electrons is transfer from metal ion to ligands and vice versa. This transition also takes place by absorbing light energy in visible region which gives color to ion.

Eg- MnO^{-4} has purple color, here electrons is transfer from O^{-2} to Mn^{+7}

CrO^{-4} is Dark Yellow

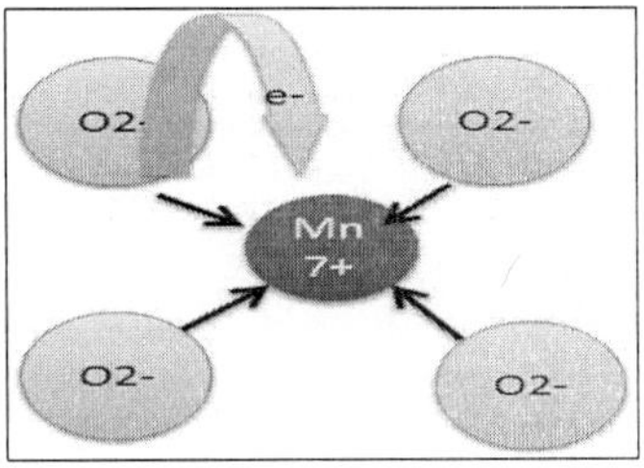

Magnetic Properties

- The magnetic properties of a metal are due to motion of electrons.
- There are two type of motion-
  a) Spin motion
  b) Orbital motion

1. Spin motion gives rise to spin moment.
2. Orbital motion gives rise to orbital moment.
3. Each electron is micro-magnet.
4. The total magnetic moment is total of magnetic moment of all electrons.
5. Therefore

   Total or effective magnetic moment = spin moment+ orbital moment

   $$\mu \text{ Effective} = \mu\text{spin} + \mu \text{ orbital}$$

6. The orbital motion of unpaired electron in d-orbital is quenched by surrounded ligands.

Therefore μ-spin is much more significant here.

Therefore,

$$\mu \text{ Effective} = \mu\text{spin} = \sqrt{n\,(n+2)}$$

Where n is no. of unpaired electrons.

7. The magnetic moment is expressed in Bohr magnetons BM

8. The magnetic moment depends on no. of unpaired electrons.

For 1 electron = $\sqrt{1(1+2)} = \sqrt{3}$ =1.73 BM

For 2 electron = $\sqrt{2(1+2)} = \sqrt{8}$ = 2.83 BM

For 3 electron = $\sqrt{3(1+3)} = \sqrt{15}$ = 3.87 BM

For 4 electron = $\sqrt{4(1+4)} = \sqrt{24}$ = 4.90 BM

For 5 electron = $\sqrt{5(1+5)} = \sqrt{35}$ = 5.92 BM

7. The magnetic moment is directly proportional to the number of unpaired electrons and it is used to find out the number of unpaired electrons.

Catalytic Properties

1. Transition elements have catalytic properties.
2. $TiCl_3$ used in Zeigler Natta catalyst for production of polythene.
3. V_2O_5 used in formation of H_2SO_4.
4. Fe is used in Haber Bosch process for making NH_3
5. $FeSO_4$ Used in Fentons reagent.
6. $PdCl_2$ useful in Wacker process.
7. Pt used in preparation of H_2SO_4.
8. Ni /Pt/Pd used in Hydrogenation of alkenes.

Chapter - 7

Metallic Bonds

- **General Properties of Metals**

  1. Metals have high electrical conductivity which decreases with increase in temperature.
  2. They good conductors of heat.
  3. They have luster, ionization energy. they are bright, shiny, highly reflective and opaque.
  4. They form crystal having high co-ordination no. of 8 or 12.
  5. They are malleable and ductile.
  6. They form crystal structure Hexagonal closed packed (hcp), body centered cubic (bcc) or face centered cubic (FCP).
  7. They form alloys.

Conductivity of Metals-

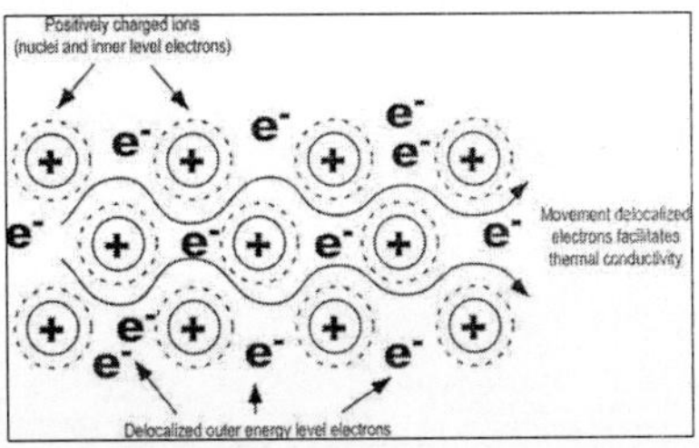

1. The high electrical conductivity of metals is due to-
   - Few electrons in valence shell
   - Vacant orbitals in valence shell
2. The electrons move in electric field and conduct electricity/heat from one to another end.
3. The electrical conductivity decreases with increase in temperature.
4. This is due the oscillation of cations in high temperature.
5. These cations hinder the movements of electrons.

6. The high thermal conductivity of metal is also due to mobile electrons.
7. The mobile electrons absorb heat and move from one end to another.

Luster

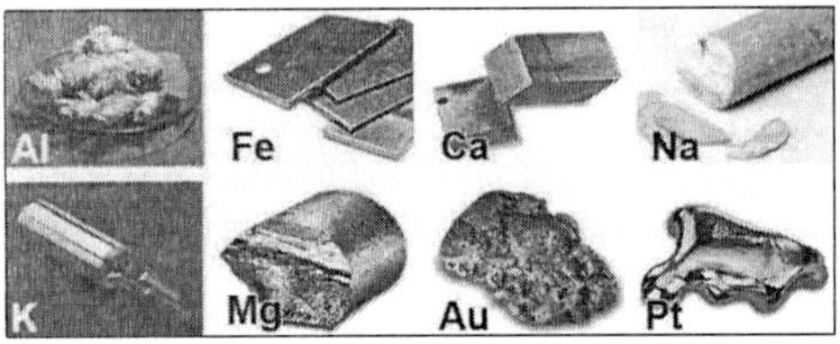

- The metal have luster. Ionization energy. they are bright, Shiny and reflective.
- This is due to free electrons.
- When white light is focused on metal surface the electrons absorbs the light energy and get excited
- This excited electrons move back to original state and electrons emit the light of particular color.
- Most of the metals are silver in color eg. Ag and Reddish and golden color of Cu and Au.
- This exchange of light gives luster to the metals.
- When metal emit electrons in light is called photoelectric effect.
- When metal emit electrons in heating is called thermionic emission.

Malleability and Ductility

- Malleability is the ability to of metal to form sheet by hammering.
- Ductility is the ability of metal to form wire.

This is due to,

- The presence of metallic bonds which are uniform in all direction.
- The metallic crystal are non-rigid.

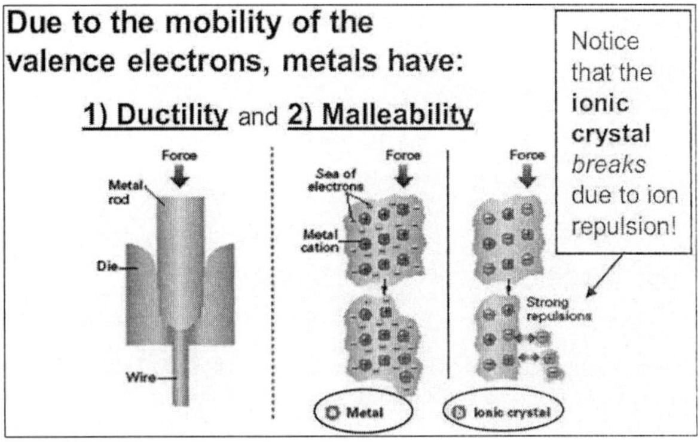

- The nearest neighbour change easily and new metallic bond can be formed.
- Metal are present in form of layers, arranged one over another.
- One layer can slide over another and free electrons can form new bond easily.

Metallic Structure and Cohesive Energy

- The cohesive energy is the force holding the atoms and ions together in the solid.
- The malleability and ductility shows that metals have large cohesive force.
- The cohesive forces are inversely proportional to internuclear distance.
- In a period, cohesive energy increases from left to right.
- There are two rules,

1. The bonding energy of metal depends on the average number of unpaired electrons. Available for bonding.
2. The crystal structures depend upon the no. of unpaired electrons in s and p orbital.

Theories of Bonding in Metals

Various theories are used in explaining bonding of metals-

- Free electron theory
- Valence bond theory
- Molecular orbital theory.

Electron Sea Model or Free Electrons Theory or Electrons Cloud Theory or Electron Gas Theory.

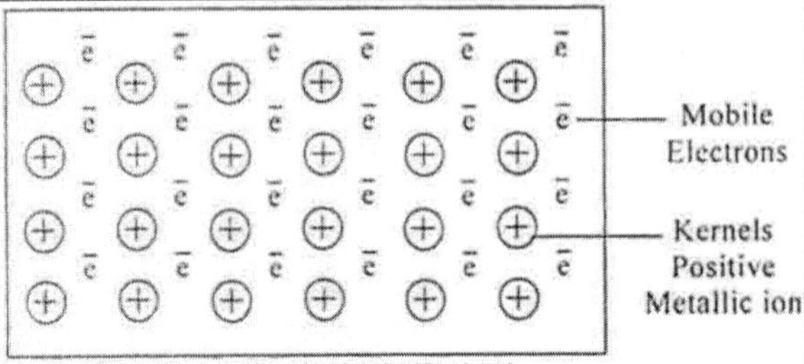

Structure of a Metallic Crystal

1. Given by Drude in 1900.
2. Under the influence of neighboring nuclei in the metallic crystal, some valence electrons of all atoms get removed and form electrons cloud or pool or gas.
3. After remove of electrons atom become positive charge and become cation (kernel).
4. These electrons are delocalized, move freely from one place to another through vacant space.
5. So the metal is network or lattice of kernels immersed in a electrons sea or pool or gas or cloud of free electrons.
6. The cohesion force is due to electrostatic force of attraction between kernels and free electrons and gives stability to the crystals.
7. The force of attraction hold the metal kernel and electrons together is called metallic bonds.
8. The electrical and thermal conductivity is due to the free electrons.

Limitations

1. It cannot explain properties of some metal-
   a) Mercury melt at low temperature
   b) (-39^{0}C) while tungsten melt at high temp. 3300^{0}C
   c) Cu is 50 times better conductor than bismuth.
   d) Sodium and potassium are so soft they cut easily by knife while osmium.
2. The calculation regarding lattice energy, specific heat, specific conductance and magnetic properties.

Valence Band Theory

1. Given by Linnaeus Pauling.
2. Metallic bond are covalent in nature.
3. Metal structure shows resonance between atoms.
4. This is possible due to vacant orbital.
5. Stability of structure increase with number of resonance structure.
6. Electrical conduction is due to presence of ions.
7. Valence shell electrons are involve in bonding.
8. Magnetic properties are due to unpaired electrons.
9. The number of bonds are depends on number of unpaired electrons.
10. E.g. Application of VBT in lithium metal-
11. It has BCC structure with 8 nearest neighbours atom.
12. Li (3) = $1S^2, 2S^2$
13. Li has one electrons in valence shell.

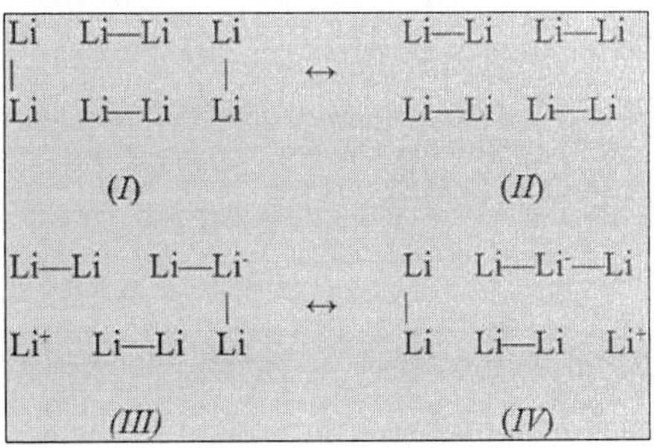

Limitations-

It is failed to -

- Explain metallic bonds in liquid state.
- Conduction of heat.
- Luster
- Semi conduction
- Decrease in conductivity with increase in temperature.

Molecular Orbital Theory

Band Theory

- The linear combination of atomic orbital gives molecular orbitals.

- The number of molecular orbital is equal to number. of atomic orbital combined
- The MO arranged according to energy level.
- Metallic bonding is due to delocalization free electrons.
- The MO is three dimensional.
- The overlap of large no. of AO forms large number of MOs which spaced closely and forms continous band called energy band.
- The band s is seperated by gaps called forbidden band.
- The band is large if greater overlapping.
- The bonding electrons are not localized at any particular atom in metal crystal, this explains malleability and ductility

Band Theory of Lithium

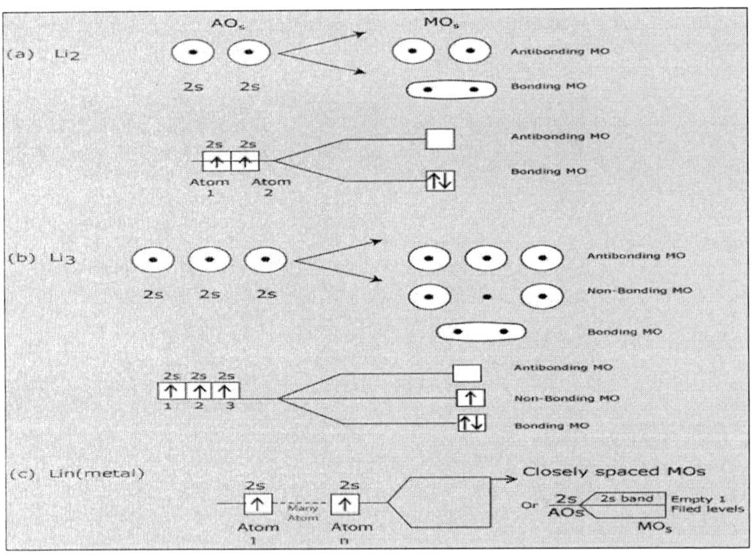

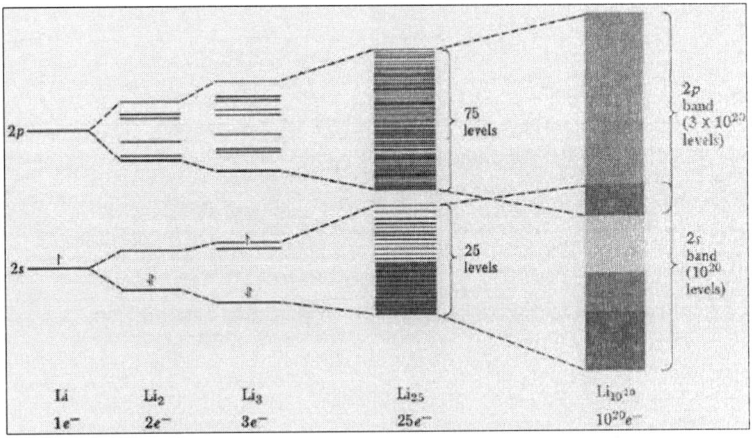

- Li (3) = 1S2, 2s1.
- Only 2s AO is involved in bonding.
- The formation of energy bands –
- **Li2** =
- The 2s AO of Li combine to form one bonding and one antibonding MO., valence electrons are entered in BMO.
- **Li 3** =
- The three 2s AO combine to forms three MO Namely BMO, NON BMO and ABMO. The 3 electrons entered in BMOs (2electrons) and NON BMO (1 electrons).
- **Li 4** =
- The four 2s AO of Li is combine to form 4MO, two BMO and 2ABMO. The four valence electrons enters in two BMO.
- **Lin** =
- The n 2S AO combine to forms n MO, n/2 BMO and N/2 ABMO. The valence electrons enter in BMO.

Band Theory of Berylium

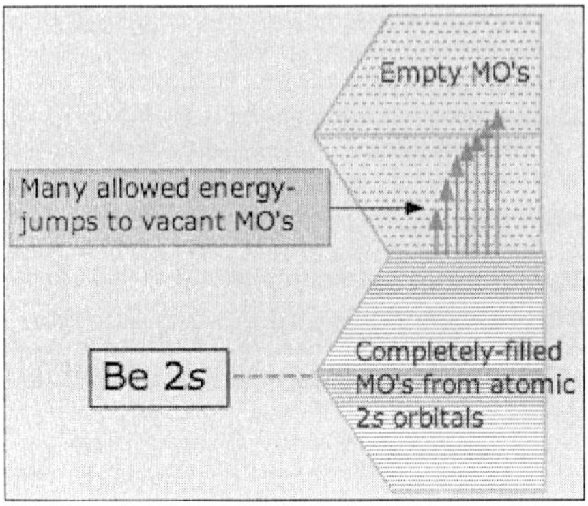

Be (4) = $1s^2, 2s^2, 2p^0$.

- The combination of 2s AO forms 2S Band.
- And 2p AO forms 2p band.
- The valence 2electrons are entered in 2S band and 2p band is empty.
- The difference in energy level of 2s and 2p is small so that 2s band and 2p band overlaps.
- Due to the overlapping of 2s and 2p, the movement of electrons from valence band to conduction band takes place.
- Thus be metal conducts heat and electricity.

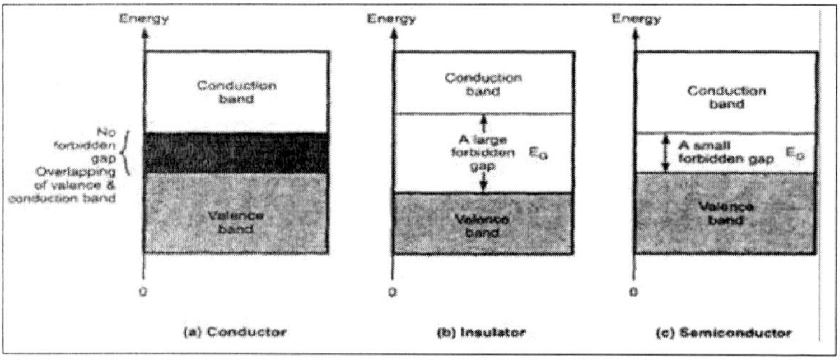

Valence band- (VB)-

- The energy band posses valence electrons are called valence band
- This band may completely filled or partially filled.
- The partially filled band can accommodate more electrons.

Conduction Band

- At ordinary temp some of valence electrons get free.
- These free electrons carry electric current, such electrons are conduction band.
- The energy band possess free electrons are called conduction band.
- If the conduction band is empty it cannot carry electric current.

Forbidden band-

- The separation between conduction band and valence band are called forbidden band.
- The greater the forbidden gap more tightly the valence electrons is held in atom.
- To move electrons from VB to CB, external energy is supplied equal to the FB energy gap.

Classification of Solids on the Basis of Band Theory

Conductors

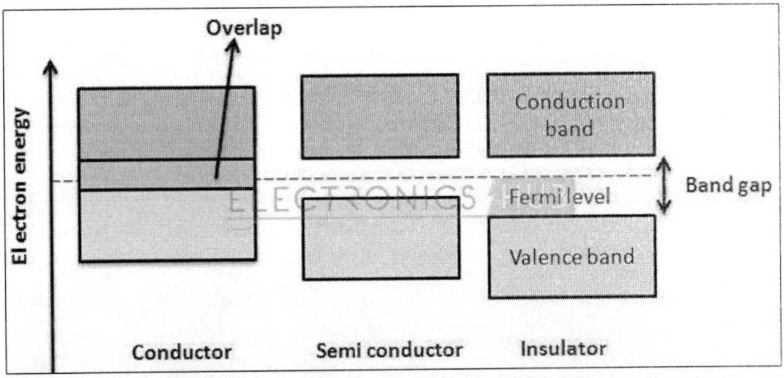

1. It is a substance with an electrical conductivity decreases with increasing temp.
2. In metal either the VB is partially filled or VB and CB is overlaps.
3. Therefore no large gap between VB and CB and movement of electrons are easily occurs.

Properties-

1. They have few electrons 1or 2.
2. VB is half filled or partially filled.

3. FB is absent.
4. Conductivity is high at room temp. And decreases with increases in temp.
5. Conductivity decreases with addition of impurity.

Insulators

1. It has zero conductivity.
2. The energy difference between VB and CB is large which make movement of electrons impossible.
3. Therefore such substance do not conduct current.
4. E.g. Nonmetal are insulators.

Properties-

1. They have large FB
2. Nonmetal having more than 4 electrons s are insulators.
3. VB is completely filled and CB is empty.
4. FB is large therefore promotion of electrons is impossible.

The conductivity cannot be increase with addition of impurity or by change in temp

Semiconductors

It is solid with low electrical conductivity that increases with increasing temp.

Properties

1. There conductivity is in between conductors and insulators.
2. Conductivity can be easily increased by addition of impurity and form n-type and p-type semiconductors.
3. There conductivity can be controlled by application of electrical field, light, pressure and heat.
4. VB is completely filled and CB is empty.
5. FB is very small.

Types of semiconductors-

1. intrinsic semiconductors
2. extrinsic semiconductors

Intrinsic Semiconductors

- It is insulators at zero temp., but become conductor at high temp.

- E.g. Graphite, germanium etc.
- On heating some electrons become free, so they can carry current.
- VB is filed and CB is empty. Therefore such Material is insulators.
- The FB is very small therefore at high temp electrons can move from VB to CB and can carry current.

Extrinsic Semiconductors

1. They are also insulators but become conductors are addition of impurities.
2. Such elements are called extrinsic semiconductors.
3. They are greater than intrinsic semiconductors.

Extrinsic Semiconductors are of two Types

1. N-type
2. P-type

- **N-Type Semiconductor**

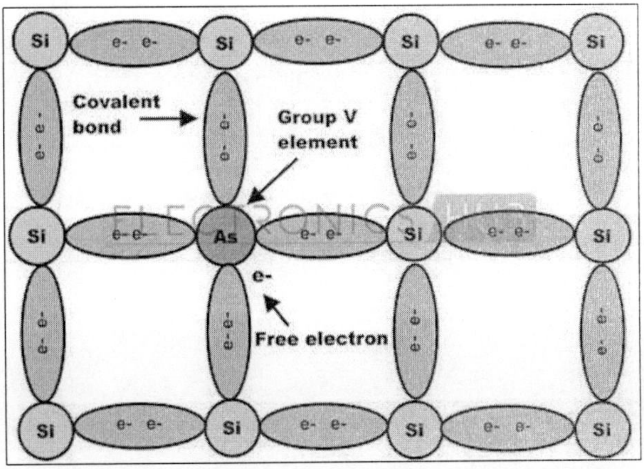

1. Conductivity is due to flow of excess electrons are called n-type semiconductors.
2. They are obtained by addition of impurity having one valence electrons more than parent atom.
3. E.g. Arsenic in silicon

   Arsenic in germanium.
4. The Arsenic has 5 valence electrons, when doped in silicon there is one electron is free which can carry current.

P-Type

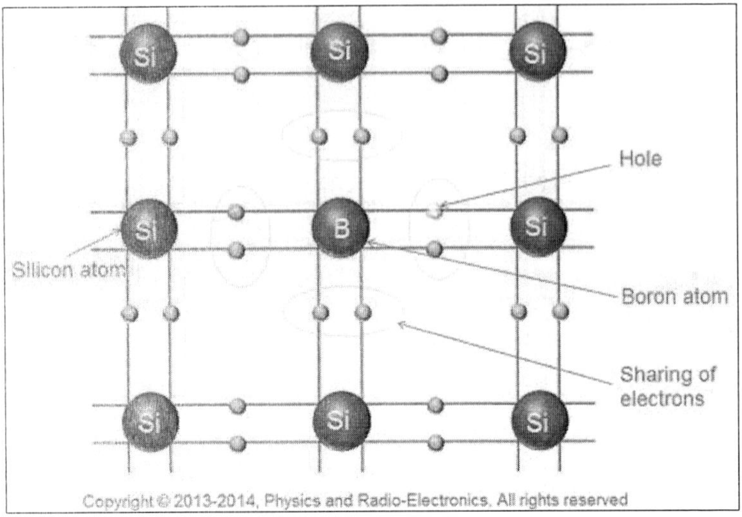

1. They show conductivity due to positive holes called p-type semiconductors.
2. They are obtained by doping with the impurity having one valence electrons less than parent atom.
3. E.g.-Doping with Ga or B in Ge
4. When B is added in Ge, B forms only three bond with Ge., this create hole in the crystal lattice, which can carry current

References

1. Concise Inorganic Chemistry by J.D. Lee. 5th Edition.
2. Theoretical Principles of Inorganic chemistry by GS Manku Tata McGraw Hill edition.
3. Advanced Inorganic Chemistry Volume-I by Satya Prakash, GD Tuli, SK Basu RD. Madan S. Chand & Company Ltd, 2004.
4. Principles of Inorganic Chemistry by Sharma, Puri Kalia 30th edition Milestone Delhi.
5. Advanced Inorganic Chemistry, by Gurdeep Raj 23rd edition, Goel Publishing House, Meerut, I.
6. A Textbook of Inorganic Chemistry by PL Soni (20th edition) (S. Chand & Sons, New Delhi.)
7. Advanced Inorganic Chemistry by Tuli, Basu, Madan & Satya Prakash - 16 Revised Edition New Delhi, 1992.
8. Principles of Physical Chemistry S. H. Maron and CF Prutton (4thedition)
9. Essentials of Physical Chemistry BS Bahl, GD Tuli, Arun Bahl (S. Chand and Co Ltd.) (25thedition)
10. Physical Chemistry Robert A. Alberty (John Willey and Sons) (7thedition)
11. A text book of Physical and Inorganic chemistry by A.M. Nemade, V.S. Zope, N.E. Barhate, R.G. Mahale, Prashant Publication.
12. http://www.bouman.chem.georgetown.edu
13. http://www.chemicol.com
14. http://www.differencebetween.net
15. http://www.electronics.howstuffworks.com
16. http://www.de.m.wikipedia.org
17. http://www.qsstudy.com